**DATE DUE**

| | | | |
|---|---|---|---|
| | | | |
| | | | |
| | | | |
| | | | |
| | | | |
| | | | |

# CONTENTS

# The Joy of Creating

Force yourself to smile and you'll soon stop frowning.

Force yourself to laugh and you'll soon find something to laugh **about**.

Wax enthusiastic and you'll very soon feel so.

A being causes **his own** feelings.

The greatest joy there is in life is creating.

Splurge on it!

L. RON HUBBARD

The bucolic Sussex countryside where L. Ron Hubbard resided from 1959 to 1966; photograph by L. Ron Hubbard

# *An Introduction to* L. Ron Hubbard

IN 1982, THROUGH THE COURSE OF A LARGER EFFORT to assemble all existing L. Ron Hubbard manuscripts, a sizeable collection of verse was discovered. Although the bulk of it dates from the 1930s, both earlier and later works suggested poetry had been a continuous pursuit and, in fact, a subsequent search through Ron's papers revealed poems from all phases of his life: youth in Montana, years of far-flung exploration, nationally acclaimed author of popular fiction and Founder of Dianetics and Scientology. That he never sought to formally present this verse, nor even spoke much of it, is immaterial. These are obviously serious poems and otherwise speak for themselves.

Presented here are more than seventy poems and songs from the L. Ron Hubbard Library. Wherever possible, relevant details have been supplied in the way of dates, circumstances and historical notes. The selection has been arranged chronologically, but is intended to be read as one wishes. For the most part, these works represent unpublished titles. That is, although he never published a body of verse per se, all ten volumes of his *Mission Earth* series offer samples of verse, as do his earlier *Ole Doc Methuselah* tales. L. Ron Hubbard poems and lyrics further saw periodic publication in various Scientology journals through the 1950s and 1960s. Then, too, a good many works herein have appeared on several musical offerings, including Ron's innovative "literary soundtracks," comprising albums to his internationally bestselling novels, *Battlefield Earth* and the *Mission Earth* series. Also herein are lyrics from his Scientology album, *The Road to Freedom,* and those albums subsequently inspired by verse and lyrics originally appearing here, including *State of Mind* and *The Joy of Creating.* Yet whether originally intended for music or latterly adapted, all stand perfectly well alone as presented through the pages to follow.

That L. Ron Hubbard left us with such a significant collection of verse comes as no

In Paris, France, 1956:
"The right way to be is to be."

surprise. After all, as a leading light of popular literature through the 1930s, he was nothing if not versatile. In addition to the reshaping of science fiction and fantasy with such perennial classics as *Fear* and *Final Blackout,* L. Ron Hubbard or one of his many pen names appeared on mysteries, westerns, aerial adventures, Far Eastern thrillers and high-sea intrigue. With the adaptation of his work for the screen in 1937, he was further author of such Hollywood serials as *The Secret of Treasure Island* and *The Adventures of the Mysterious Pilot.* He was still further a lifelong musician, composer and songwriter. While throughout and overall, as award-winning author-critic Catherine L. Moore declared, there is something akin to poetry in every page

from L. Ron Hubbard—specifically "the skill to do more, with the will to refrain."

Finally, no introduction to the poems of L. Ron Hubbard is complete without mention of how poetry figured into his greater trail of research to the founding of Dianetics and Scientology: in particular, his 1931 experimentation revealing verse as a universally recognized aesthetic and thus a common denominator between otherwise divergent peoples. Needless to say, the trail was long, the vista immense and the details fascinating. (It seems he found tangible links between metered rhythm and the rhythm of life.) But as poetry was itself a lifelong pursuit, let us consider his life as a poet. ◼

My own
verse is usually
free verse.
The freer
the better.

# EARLY VERSE

# Early Verse

ALTHOUGH BORN IN TILDEN, NEBRASKA, IN 1911, it was the heartland of Montana that L. Ron Hubbard first called home. Of his youth in the state capital of Helena, he wrote: "I lived in the typical West with its do-and-dare attitudes, its wry humor, cowboy pranks and make nothing of the worst and most dangerous."

If a generally harsh and rude world, however, the Hubbard family home was by no means culturally deprived. Under the tutelage of his mother, a former schoolteacher, Ron was reading by the age of three and a half, and had soon digested whole shelves of classics. He was also writing by an early age, and a canvas-bound accountant's ledger is filled with both diary sketches and fragments of short stories. Likewise scattered throughout are early bits of verse.

As a word on these early works, he tells of first experimenting with free verse in about 1927, to entertain the younger children of a visiting admiral, "and I learned from that, actually, the simplicity of the rendition; there's nothing contrived about free verse if you're really writing it in a free style." In an apt description, he then spoke of the form as "not quite logical,

*Left* In Washington, DC, 1924: a young Ron Hubbard begins filling notebooks with a first body of verse

but aesthetic," adding, it has "a very, very broad general appeal."

The particulars of that appeal became the subject of a very definite study four years later when an engineering student at George Washington University. Utilizing a now curious device known as the Koenig photometer, he succeeded in diagraming what inventor Karl Rudolph Koenig (1832–1901) had described as "sound figures" characteristic of spoken vowels, i.e., a diagrammatic imprint of human voice. What Ron found he described as "the aesthetic of language" and noted that spoken

verse, regardless of language, left precisely the same imprint on the photometer. That is, a poem read in English—he specifically tested the works of Robert Browning—left the same rhythmical imprint in terms of vowels and consonants as Japanese haiku or an Indian hymn. In other words, the essence of poetry is universal. Moreover, it is recognizable as such regardless of whether one speaks the language. How exactly we are able to identify this "aesthetic of language" became a question of immense ramifications and involved a line of research that would carry him through the next two decades. Nevertheless, poetry in and of itself was not soon forgotten.

Ron's own verse from the early 1920s and 1930s is of two types. Initially, of course, there was his free verse, typified by "The Sum of Man" and "Cold, Wet Decks," reprinted here. The first, as the title implies, offers an incisive view of what makes up the emotional canvas of a human being and is among those works found in Ron's earliest diary—specifically that accountant's ledger apparently appropriated from his maternal grandfather.

The second, "Cold, Wet Decks," would seem to have been inspired by an LRH short story from the same period entitled *Grounded*. Appearing in the George Washington University *Literary Review* of April 1932, it tells of an embittered Royal Air Force pilot on an existential journey up the Yangtze in prerevolutionary China. The story was years ahead of commensurate undergraduate work and drawn from Ron's own extensive travels through a war-torn China. In any case, "Cold, Wet Decks" serves as a kind of free verse synopsis.

Also included are two early ballads: "Custer's Second Chance" and "The Sailors." The first is reflective of a longtime LRH love—Native American heritage. Blood brother to the Blackfeet and keen student of Indian ways, Ron was eventually to author one of the era's only accurate and sympathetic novels of the Native American experience, his 1937 *Buckskin Brigades*. He was also one of the first to conduct an ethnological study of the Pacific Northwest tribes, while his appreciation of shamanic rites was decades ahead of its time. Although General George Armstrong Custer's demise represented neither a high point for the United States Cavalry nor the Sioux Nation—the Little Bighorn actually signaled the beginning of their end—Custer's last stand nonetheless loomed large in many a Western youth's mind. In all probability, the work dates from March of 1924, when a rail trip from the nation's capital to Helena, Montana, took the thirteen-year-old

L. Ron Hubbard very nearly through the Little Bighorn Valley.

"The Sailors" is likewise reflective of a lifelong love, in this case, seafaring lore. Quite possibly penned that same year in Seattle, Washington, the work says much about the young L. Ron Hubbard's world. With his father serving as Supply Officer at the United States Naval Yard at Bremerton, and otherwise surrounded by things nautical, Ron was acutely conscious of what the early twentieth century meant in terms of seafaring advances; hence, his two ancient sailors "Who told of harder, wetter days on small and dirty whalers." ■

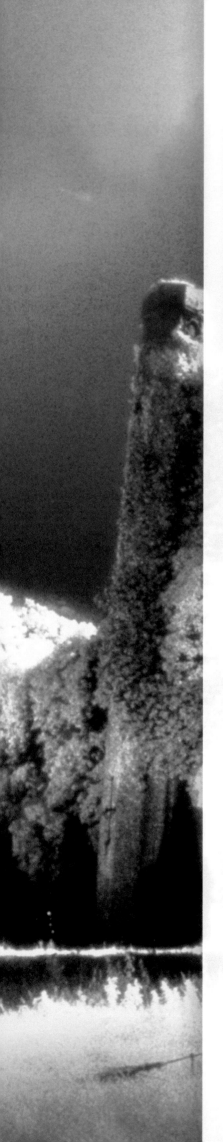

## The Sum of Man

*Although undated, diary entries surrounding "The Sum of Man" suggest it was written through the early 1920s—or when Ron was still in his teens. In that regard, the work stands as among his earliest efforts at free verse, and an extraordinary one.*

# THE SUM OF MAN

(Featured on L. Ron Hubbard's The Joy of Creating album)

★ ★ ★

## PASSION

*Swirling*
*Ivory thoughts*
*Steeped*
*In red-flecked*
*Blackness*

★ ★ ★

## AMBITION

*Fire*
*Burning—searing*
*Torturing*
*My tied hands*

★ ★ ★

## CONCEIT

*Houses perched*
*On stenching*
*Quicksand*

★ ★ ★

## CONSCIENCE

*Racking sobs*
*Of*
*A heart*
*Which cannot cry*

★ ★ ★

## FEAR

*Black soul*
*Naked*
*To*
*A shrieking wind*

★ ★ ★

## HYPOCRISY

*Sleek—*
*Dripping with*
*An*
*Inner oil*
*Which rots*

★ ★ ★

## TEMPER

*Cramming pity*
*Of*
*A blurred mind*

★ ★ ★

## CUPIDITY

*Unclean Lancet*
*Unnerving*
*The eye*

★ ★ ★

## JEALOUSY

*Swaying Towers*
*Prey*
*To a zephyr*

★ ★ ★

## HATE

*Unspoken words*
*Carrion*
*To nauseate*
*And Snarl*
*The guts.*

# COLD, WET DECKS

*Cold, wet decks*
*Creeping dawn*
*The gentle whirr of engines*
*Swishing yellow waters*
*The Yang-tze-kiang*
*Kowtung Gorge*
*Yellow walls*
*Yellow sky*
*Cruel yellow rapids*
*Sneering, hideous rapids*
*Waiting, waiting to crush*
*The gunboat.*

*A crouched figure.*
*Shivering, watching.*
*A blue figure,*
*The lookout*
*Silent, half blind.*
*Pulling hungrily at a cigarette*
*Watching, watching the dawn.*

*Cold, wet decks.*
*The brittle fingers of the helmsman.*
*The smarting eyes of the pilot*
*The yellow gorge*
*The yellow waters.*

*The sudden crash of musketry.*
*Whirling yellow men on the banks*
*An alarm gong,*
*The whimper of the lookout*
*The hysterical laugh of a machine gun.*

# CUSTER'S SECOND CHANCE

*A plain, milk white with moonlight,*
*A pencil line of Buttes.*
 *A cayuse munchin' grass quite near,*
*Snappin' it off at the roots.*
 *A coyote mourned a long lost love,*
*With soulful notes of bass*
 *And I lay and stared at the sky above,*
*Let the moonlight bathe my face.*

 *The plain was ringed by fantasy,*
*The ghosts of years gone by,*
 *Came sneakin' from their daylight haunts*
*With footsteps soft and shy.*
 *A man that looked like Custer*
*Stood at my heaving side.*
 *"Oho my man," the vision said,*
*"Why beneath your covers hide?*

 *"Get up, get up, don't lie and groan,*
*We're friends of yours I swear!*
 *Arise and shine, me bucko.*
*Get out of your wooly lair.*
 *'For the Sioux are here, hi they whoop.*
*Our ammunition's low*
 *They burn the wagon trains of whites.*
*Their war dance fires glow."*

 *I sat up straight, pulled on my boots,*
*And said to the Spirit, bold,*
 *"See here, old chap, I've read of you*
*And your lances that grow cold.*
 *Upon the banks of a quiet stream,*
*Beneath a summer's sun.*
 *And how you fought old Sittin' Bull,*
*And your men fell one by one."*

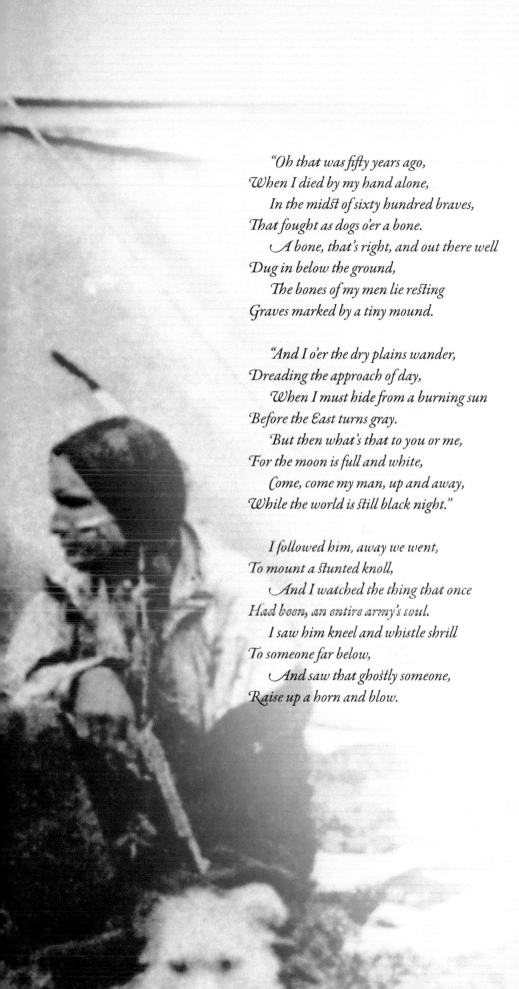

"Oh that was fifty years ago,
When I died by my hand alone,
    In the midst of sixty hundred braves,
That fought as dogs o'er a bone.
    A bone, that's right, and out there well
Dug in below the ground,
    The bones of my men lie resting
Graves marked by a tiny mound.

"And I o'er the dry plains wander,
Dreading the approach of day,
    When I must hide from a burning sun
Before the East turns gray.
    But then what's that to you or me,
For the moon is full and white,
    Come, come my man, up and away,
While the world is still black night."

I followed him, away we went,
To mount a stunted knoll,
    And I watched the thing that once
Had been, an entire army's soul.
    I saw him kneel and whistle shrill
To someone far below,
    And saw that ghostly someone,
Raise up a horn and blow.

A weird, sweet quaver. Assembly,
To which a throng replied,
    And ringed us round, and stared at me,
And at the man beside.
    "To horse, to boots and saddles,
Advance! Squadrons right!"
    And away we flew, quite silent,
Into a boundless night.

    Far off a fire flickered, danced,
From far off came a yell,
    A scattering blast of musketry,
But not a trooper fell.
    Bolt upright with sabers
Drawn, and "on parade,"
    Troop on troop, in column,
Then the phantom bugle brayed.

    The sabers all came down "to charge"
The dancing fire neared,
    And Indians, by the thousand,
All kneeling unafeared.
    Through their line, once and twice,
We charged, and then again,
    The savage lines broke and ran,
And left to us, their slain.

    The general, silent at my side,
Smiled at his men in praise,
    And they looked back at him and grinned,
Each hand to cap did raise.
    The bugle whimpered out tattoo
For the East was turning gray,
    A coyote howled a mournful note
To curse the coming day.

*The ranks about wheeled sharply,*
*An echo, they were gone,*
*The man beside glanced fearfully*
*Toward the approaching dawn.*
*Then he too, wheeled his steed*
*And cried to me, "farewell."*
*I looked and watched him speed away,*
*To hide from daylight's hell.*

*Back to my camp, I turned my horse,*
*And crawled into my bed,*
*To gain such sleep as I could get,*
*E're the East turned red.*
*I slept, I know, into the day,*
*For the sun was up on high,*
*I squirmed about and tried to think,*
*Of where I was and why.*

*I sat upright and placed my hand,*
*'Where a rusty saber lay.*
*I picked it up with some surprise*
*And fingered its decay.*
*I read thereon, the time dimmed words,*
*Custer, '74.*
*I read and stared, and creased my brow,*
*Recalled what had gone before.*

*I looked to my guns, found grime and dirt,*
*Inspected my lathered horse,*
*And felt a panic snatch at me,*
*To direct from there my course.*
*My horse got saddled awry,*
*My pack, I let it lay,*
*And left the fearsome plain behind,*
*My courage turned to clay.*

# THE SAILORS

*I rolled along the littered dock*
*And met two ancient sailors*
*Who told of harder, wetter days*
*On small and dirty whalers.*
*Then one of the salts asked the other one*
*If he knew aught of afterlife*
*And the other growled in his deep bass voice*
*And let his words run rife.*

*"Have ye ever stood on a heavin' deck,*
*And watched the white caps race.*
*And heard the riggin' whine and moan*
*And spring sure after brace?*
*Have ye ever watched the scuppers roll,*
*Hard under and alee?*
*Then ye know what hell is!*

*"Have ye ever hoisted, stiff with ice,*
*A mainsul, cold and white,*
*And broke yer knuckles and yer nails*
*'Fixin' the aft truck light?*
*And damn near cried with the*
*Searing pain chasing over ye?*
*Then ye know what hell is.*

*"Have ye ever stood the midnight dog,*
*And fought a writhin' wheel?*
*And called aloft the starboard watch*
*T' keep water on her keel?*
*Have ye ever heard the lightning crash,*
*And take away the main?*
*Then ye know what hell is.*

*"But then, I ask, have ye heard,*
*An evening curlew's cry,*
*And felt a gracious tropic rain*
*And heard the south wind sigh?*
*And have ye seen a yellow moon,*
*Ease up into the sky?*
*Then ye know what heaven is.*

*"And have ye heard with yer own ears,*
*A siren's pleading song?*
*And had a foreign maiden, hold*
*That horny hand o'er long?*
*And sipped the lotus of the south,*
*Where labor can't belong?*
*Then ye know what heaven is."*

*And then he stopped and noticed me*
*And looked at me quite sad.*
*"That makes you long for a sailor's life*
*For ye look none so glad*
*But never be a sailor-man,*
*Just study yer lessons, lad,*
*And ye'll know what earth is."*

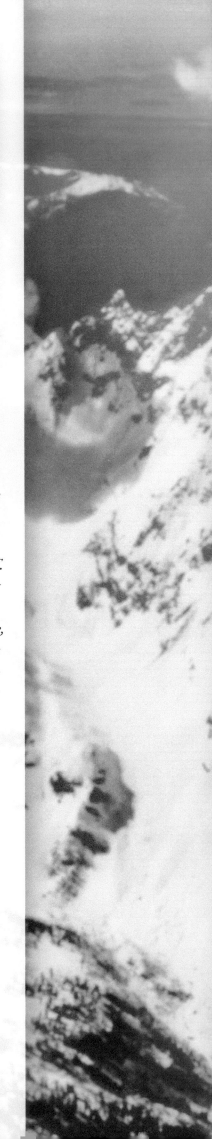

## Above It All

*In the spring of 1928, in what amounted to the start of his second Asia journey, a seventeen-year-old L. Ron Hubbard set out from his home in Helena, Montana, with little more than the clothes in his knapsack and the proceeds from the sale of an old Model T. To increase his meager funds, he briefly signed on as a Boy Scout instructor at Washington's Camp Parsons above Puget Sound. From Camp Parsons, he next set out across the Olympic Mountains where, as noted in his diary, "...that night, I made camp about two miles down trail from 'Shelter Rock.' Twelve hours later, I was limp on top of a boulder pile, saved from a broken spine by my pack." Presumably before that near-fatal fall, however, he also penned "Above It All."*

# ABOVE IT ALL

(Featured on L. Ron Hubbard's State of Mind album)

High on a sun-bathed peak I trod
    Through granite rocks and snow
Below me lay the world.
    Tiring, I sat pensive on
A rough gray monster of stone
    A fresh, cool wind bathed
My earth tired brain.
    'Neath my feet lay
The farms.
    All squared with wheat and hay
Light green against dark
    Tan against brown.
Detached—my mind reasoned.

# BLUE ENDLESS SEA

(Featured on L. Ron Hubbard's The Joy of Creating album)

Blue, endless sea,
Stretching, lazy, to the horizon,
Wreckage, a floating spar,
A capsized lifeboat,
A life jacket,
Grey fins ripping the water,
Grey triangles, searching.

A raft, dipping, swaying
A man.
Sitting head in hands,
Watching, watching the horizon.
The sun, white hot, spinning.

A blue sky and miles of sea.
Blue endless sea
Stretching to the horizon, forever,
The man, watching.
A grey fin, hoping.

A tiny smudge of black,
Smoke of a steamer.
The man blinks, opens his mouth,
Screaming joy.
The smoke enlarges,
The man, half mad, dancing
The smoke fading,
Growing smaller,
Disappearing.

Blue endless sea,
Stretching lazy to the horizon,
Wreckage.
A man sitting head in hands,
Watching, watching the horizon,
The sun white hot, spinning,
A blue sky and miles of sea.

## The Castaway Song

*Dating from the mid-1920s and a first Pacific crossing, "The Castaway Song" is all that remains of a lost operatic work. Some five decades later, however, Ron composed a melody for the song. Consequently, lyrics and music can now be heard on the State of Mind album as performed by Scientology's Golden Era Musicians.*

# THE CASTAWAY SONG

(FEATURED ON L. RON HUBBARD'S STATE OF MIND ALBUM)

*Morning ever greets my weary eyes*

*With naught but rolling sea*

*Tossing endless miles of white-capped waves*

*Haunting, mocking me*

*Roll on, roll on, roll on*

*Thou cruel and leering sea*

*Roll on, roll on, roll on*

*To God that I were free*

*You hold me chained 'neath white and burning suns*

*What could you want with me?*

*Oh God, can't someone hear my castaway song?*

*No, no one but the sea*

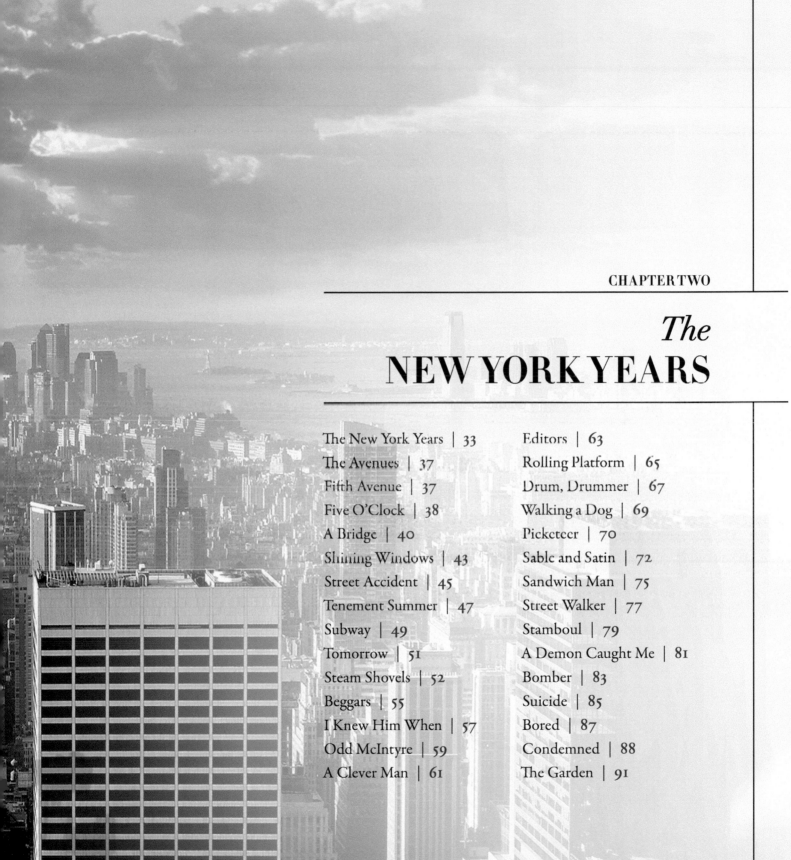

# *The* NEW YORK YEARS

# The
# New York Years

FTER SEVERAL YEARS OF FAR-FLUNG travel—through Asia, the South Pacific and across the Caribbean—L. Ron Hubbard settled into a beachfront cottage in Encinitas, California, where, as he put it, "I took things out of my mind and wrote them into stories." Initially, of course, the challenge proved considerable, and only those who attempted to "click with fiction" through the early 1930s can appreciate the strain of facing a blank page at the height of the Great Depression. Yet setting himself on a regimen "to pile up copy, stack up stories, roll the wordage," he did indeed click with fiction. His first acceptance was a nicely wrought formula piece entitled *The Green God,* loosely drawn from experiences in China. Then, following the sale of two high adventures and a mystery, he set out for that mecca which has always beckoned writers, New York City.

He arrived in the spring of 1935 to join a fairly legendary circle of authors, including Edgar Rice Burroughs, Lester "Doc Savage" Dent and Norvell "The Spider" Page. Their primary vehicle was the equally legendary pulps. So called for the pulpwood stock on which they were printed and generally appearing monthly, these fiercely competitive magazines were easily the most popular publications of their day. As a matter of fact, with some thirty million regular readers—a full quarter of the American population—only television would finally rival the pulps in terms of sheer appeal. But make no mistake, if the pulps were unashamedly popular, they were by no means pedestrian.

In addition to the likes of Dent and Burroughs, both Raymond Chandler and Dashiell Hammett wrote for the pulps and much of what marks modern American literature as lean and hard-boiled may be traced to those pulpwood pages.

The stamp L. Ron Hubbard left would finally prove just as enduring. Enlisted by pulp magnate Street & Smith to help boost sagging sales of *Astounding Science Fiction,* he was soon authoring works that would effectively reshape

An undisputed King of the Great Pulp Jungle, New York City, 1940

the genre whole cloth—humanize it, break it out of a mechanical mold and so cut a wake through all we know of modern science fiction. No less influential were L. Ron Hubbard's tales of fantasy, including the perennially applauded *Fear, Slaves of Sleep* and *Typewriter in the Sky*—all works that continue to resonate across imaginative literature and thereby imbue the genre with strains of great pulp music.

His verse, albeit a lesser melody, is woven throughout. The earliest samples appear handwritten on sheets of American Fiction Guild stationery. (Ron served as president of the Guild's New York chapter from 1935 to 1936, in which capacity he lobbied tirelessly on behalf of the up-and-coming author.) In the main, the imagery is drawn from the world around him. New York City circa 1935, he would remark, had been nothing if not alive: "Hectic and noisy and quarrelsome and confusing, but terrific." His verse reflects the same with etched images of subways, skyscrapers, sandwich men and garment workers. That much of what he sees is ironic or faintly pitiful is to be expected. After all, this was still a Manhattan in the grip of depression. Hence: "White collars walking for lunch money," worn shoes hidden beneath a chair, and the gaze that could not be met "because I had a coat and he had none."

Those who would additionally see parallels between Ron's works and Chinese verse—particularly as translated by American

imagist founder Ezra Pound—are not far off. In fact, Ron was much taken with T'ang dynasty master Po Chü-i, who so influenced the likes of Pound and William Carlos Williams. (It is Po, for example, whom Ron references in his text *ART* when speaking of the Chinese master who would publish nothing unless "approved" by the corner flower lady.) But Ron's use of a solitary image with Asian brevity was not derived from the imagists. Rather, having spent two critical years in Asia and actually studied both Japanese and Chinese dialects, he was legitimately tapping the source of the modernist trend. Otherwise he experimented with older Western forms, notably the romantic and medieval. As a word on such experimentation, he tells of intentionally pushing the pulp envelope with tenth- to sixteenth-century cadences. That the stories sold, he explains, "didn't prove too much because I never had any trouble with that. But that they were understood at all was surprising to me, for their prose types (ranging from *Shakespeare* to *Beowulf*) were at wild variance with anything currently being published." In terms of verse, the same employment of the archaic yielded such hauntingly formal works as "The Garden" and "Tomorrow." In either case, as he elsewhere remarked, "all kinds of lines keep rambling through my mind." ◾

## THE AVENUES

The avenues
Have cavalry
Charging to attack.

The avenues
Have cannons,
Infantry,
And tanks.

The side streets
Have
Hospitals.

## FIFTH AVENUE

Green beetles
Snarling.
A dime.

Yellow bees
Darting.
Twenty and Five.

Black caskets
Purring
No price.

White collars
Walking
'For
Lunch money.

They built
Upon
An island

But
You never
see
the sea.

# FIVE O'CLOCK

*Noise*
*And Hurry.*
*Jarring*
*Sound*
*Blare*
*And scurry*
*Whither*
*Bound?*

# A BRIDGE

*A bridge*
*That swings*
*Above*
*A stream*

*A high proud bridge*
*with cables*

*A bridge which leads*
*Away*
*From there to*
*Green and red far shores*

*A bridge which has*
*A sign*
*Which says*
*"Foot passengers five cents."*

# SHINING WINDOWS

*Shining windows*
*In*
*The sun*
*Tall,*
*Tall buildings*
*Staring.*

*Sell*
*and buy*
*and*
*Sell*
*and buy.*

*Monuments*
*Those buildings.*
*Eyes*
*Those windows*
*Watching.*

*Prisons, too,*
*Have*
*Windows.*

# STREET ACCIDENT

The cab
Played
Hopscotch
With the poles.

The cabbie
gnawed
A dead cigar.

The man
Saws signs
With listless eyes.

The cab
Slid by
A halting
Bus.

In all
That clamor
How small
The sound.

In all
That crowd
Eyes
Only stared.

An Irish
Cop
Kept them away.

The ambulance
Swallowed
with
Satisfied clang.

The cabbie
Put
His card
away.
And saw
Two upturned shoes.

The man
With listless eyes.
Again
Watched signs.

# TENEMENT SUMMER

*Hot*
*So that*
*Iron burned.*

*Hot*
*So that*
*Asphalt*
*Fried.*

*Hot*
*So that*
*Children*
*White.*

*From*
*Yard to yard*
*Faded*
*Clothing*
*Fluttered.*

*Like*
*Pennons*
*in*
*The Fleet.*

*Futile and trapped.*
*All energy sapped*
*And sitting on a quay.*

*Longing and thinking.*

## Subway

*In addition to those stories drawn from earlier adventures in Asia, the Caribbean and South Pacific, Ron was forever plunging into extreme situations in search of new grist for his literary mill. Case in point was his research for the 1936–1937 "Hell Job" series, focusing upon the world's most dangerous professions. In the name of such research, he variously scaled precarious heights with steeplejacks, explored the bottom of Puget Sound with deep-sea divers and stunted with daredevil pilots.*

*His adventure at the controls of a New York subway represented more of the same. For a possible story involving an underground tragedy, he found himself behind the throttle as "Hissing grinding, / Destiny thrust it / On its way."*

# SUBWAY

oar.
Grinding wheels.
Charge, clang, roar.
A big steel mole
Snarls through the gloom.

Ten thousand dentists,
Ten thousand drills
On ten thousand teeth.

Roar, roar,
It's slowing
How it hates to slow!
Grudging hiss
Of pent and compressed breath.
It even hates to breathe.

Rush.
The engineer
In gloomy cab
Strains his glove
Over throttle.
Pugnacious engineer,
Anxious as the train
To be away.

Drills again
And sway and lurch.
The platform crowd
Has changed.
Hissing grinding,
Destiny thrust it
On its way.

Purpose which
breeds envy to
Such as I.

# TOMORROW

Tomorrow
To that place
I came again
To witness
Destiny.

It could not pause
But with
its grudging
Hiss it paused
in
Enforced idleness.

I saw
The engineer
With same set face
On same hard track
With same gloved hand...

And
Tomorrow....

# STEAM SHOVELS

*Steam shovels*
*Should*
*Be pretty things.*

*Steam shovels*
*Should*
*Be more.*

*When all things*
*come*
*To an end at last*
*It is*
*quite good*
*To stand*
*with pockets filled*
*with fingers and*

*watch*
*Steam shovels.*

# BEGGARS

*Brother*
*Could you spare*
*A dime?*

*Brother?*
*Did he say.*

*He*
*Didn't know*
*The lining of*
*My overcoat*
*Is torn.*

*Brother?*
*Yes*
*And higher up*
*I say*
*"Please*
*I need*
*The raise."*

# I KNEW HIM WHEN

*The wine was good.*
*I knew him when.*
*He had a flight of steps.*

*He had a maid*
*He had three cars*
*He had a wife with lorgnette.*

*The wine was good,*
*I knew him when.*
*But shoes are hid beneath my*
*    chair*
*My tie is tied*
*Where it is worn*
*My shirt had sleeves*
*My coat....*

*The wine was good*
*So was his face*
*I knew him when, you see.*

*But guests were coming*
*And I stood*
*And listened*
*Across from those*
*Lighted windows.*

*You see*
*I only knew him when.*

## Odd McIntyre

*In March of 1936, New York columnist and critic Oscar Odd McIntyre leveled four acerbic inches of copy at what he described as "a weird offshoot of magazine publishing," i.e., the pulps. His criticism was stock, superficial and actually untrue, as in: "Every possible historic plot has been catalogued, and copies are furnished a group of writers who punch the clock like factory hands." There were no pulp factories, writers certainly received no hourly wages, and if plot lines seemed classical, it was only because all competent stories tend to echo classical themes. It was, however, true that those fortunate enough to make the pulp grade tended to command hefty salaries and certainly wrote more than the 800 words a day penned by the likes of McIntyre.*

*As president of the American Fiction Guild's New York chapter, and highly visible master of popular fiction, L. Ron Hubbard was called upon to supply a response. That response, in the form of a 2,500-word article entitled "Pulpateer" is as truthful as McIntyre's is not. "Primarily, a pulpateer is a very decent writer (he has to be that, you know). He is sincere about his work as any of the top rankers will testify. He tries to write his very best and make his stories exciting and often he gets a lot more than excitement into them." By the same token, however, and given the two-fisted reputation of pulpateers, Ron felt obliged to wryly add: "If you should happen to intimate to a pulpateer that his stories are trash, you are likely to be soundly punched in the nose." In either case, the eventual meeting with this O. O. McIntyre inspired an altogether subtler response.*

# ODD McINTYRE

*I saw him there,*
*I held my breath.*
*And tried to feel at ease.*

*I knew*
*you know*
*That he was he*
*And that each day*
*His words,*
*you see*
*Were strung out in*
*a column of*
*influential ink.*

*I knew*
*you know*
*His words and that*
*He made a man*
*with just a few*
*Typewriter taps.*

*I saw him there.*
*I was afraid.*
*And then*
*you see*
*He rose.*
*His fingers shook*
*you know*
*Because*
*He*
*was*
*afraid.*

# A CLEVER MAN
(FEATURED ON L. RON HUBBARD'S STATE OF MIND ALBUM)

*A clever man—*
*Not me—*
*Was born on a purple spread*
*And learned at a tutor's clerkly knee—*
*Not me—*
*A clever man—*
*Not me—*
*Took sheepskin at a proper school*
*Employment in the family—*
*Not me—*
*A clever man—*
*Not me—*
*Married a highly dowered bride*
*Got children and much property—*
*Not me—*
*A clever man—*
*Not me—*
*Minus boots with his family round*
*Died at comfortable seventy—*
*Not me.*
*A clever man—*
*Not me—*
*Tasted none of the bitter sins*
*Valued his placidity—*
*Not me!*

## Editors

*For all the pulps finally yielded in terms of memorable fiction, those who wrote for the likes of Argosy or Thrilling Adventures were not without complaints. Of particular irritation were constraining editorial policies. "I am and have been for years a good craftsman,"* Ron very truthfully conceded, *"but the very things I possess such as originality and inventiveness are not tools to the magazine trade."*

*His point is well taken, and is actually echoed in the memoirs of several who wrote for the pulps—which is not to suggest pulp authors and editors were routinely at odds; Ron himself counted several as close friends, even including the famously irascible science fiction editor John W. Campbell, Jr. By the same token, however, his incisive "Editors" says much.*

# EDITORS

*M*en will come
Along this blaze hacked
by pen in wilderness
Of fact.

Men will come
And in coming scowl and utter
thunderous wrath
And say that here and HERE
A comma is out of place.

# ROLLING PLATFORM

*He had*
*A rolling platform*
*Filled*
*With coats.*

*A taxi*
*Honked*
*And hurried*
*By.*

*He crossed*
*The street,*
*And pushed*
*His cart*
*Aside.*

*Before he entered*
*With his coats*
*He*
*Took off*
*His cheap rings.*

*He kissed*
*Her cheek*
*Most tenderly*
*And put*
*Back on his hat.*

*She looked*
*At him*
*And then*
*Her chauffeur*
*Drove away.*

*I wonder*
*Why*
*He bought*
*That rose before*
*He vanished*
*in*
*His building.*

## Drum, Drummer

*Comprising yet another selection on the State of Mind album, the musical rendition of "Drum, Drummer" features vocals from rock legend Edgar Winter. While for another word on the soul of a drummer, Ron writes: "He has to be with it in every fiber of his being...it requires a certain surrender of self to the beat."*

# DRUM, DRUMMER

(Featured on L. Ron Hubbard's State of Mind album)

*Drum, drummer, drum!*
  *Flash, lights*
  *Smile, girls.*
*Drum, drummer, drum!*

  *Blare, trombone, blare*
  *Dance, women,*
  *Laugh, men*
*Drum, drummer, drum.*

*Scrape, fiddles, scrape*
  *Swing, dancers*
  *Shine, glasses*
*Drum, drummer, drum.*

*Wah, trumpets, wah!*
  *Slide, penguins*
  *Clash, bodies.*
*Drum, drummer, drum!*

# WALKING A DOG

*Why does she lead
That
Pampered dog?*

*She
Waits
And tugs
His leash.*

*She
Has a round
And
Childish face.
She
Has lovely eyes.*

# PICKETEER

*The picketeer*
*Was strolling*
*Before the mighty doors.*

*A picketeer*
*Was cold.*

*A picketeer*
*looked at*
*The cop.*

*A picketeer*
*was strolling*
*and behind*
*The fine*
*plate windows*

*A small man*
*wrung*
*His pudgy*
*Hands.* *Ron*

# SABLE AND SATIN

Mercedes-Benz
at
The curb.

A
Doorman
who bowed
His
Stiff head.

An
Escort
in
Penguin
Full Dress.

A
Chauffeur
who knew
She
Had obscene eyes. *Ron*

# SANDWICH MAN

*He had*
*His hands*
*Under the straps.*

*It banged*
*In a dusty*
*Wind.*

*His ice blue fingers*
*Trembled when*
*He lifted*
*His shabby*
*Collar.*

*His sign,*
*Which dragged*
*About his neck*
*Cried,*
*"Overcoats*
*Gloves."*

*I wouldn't watch*
*His eyes because*
*I had*
*A coat and he had none.*

# STREET WALKER

She
Was small
And round.
She
Had been
Younger,
Healthier.

She
Walked
Slower
and slower
Until
We were both
In shadow.

She
Didn't say
a word.
She
Only looked
A little,
Hopelessly.

I went on
And wondered
If,
She was hungry.

## Stamboul & A Demon Caught Me

*Of particular prevalence through L. Ron Hubbard fantasy of 1939 and 1940 is the highly intriguing notion of modern Man still in the grip of primeval superstition. His most realized rendering of the theme is, of course, Fear, telling of an American ethnologist tormented by the contrary spirits he had examined as quaint superstition. And yet, as the doomed professor James Lowry must finally declare: "We are intelligent beings, giving our lips to disbelief, but rolling our eyes behind us to search out any danger which might swoop down from that black void." In the same vein, and from the same period, is "A Demon Caught Me" to remind us that "Black cats, stepladders and horseshoes are whirled—amid life which hard cling the material world."*

*To accommodate such LRH works of pure fantasy as Fear and The Ultimate Adventure, the publishing magnate of Street & Smith launched the all-fantasy Unknown. In a definitive word on the genre, Ron described fantasy as "any fiction that takes up elements such as spiritualism, mythology, magic, divination, the supernatural, and so on." (In contrast, he explains, science fiction must rest upon the scientifically feasible.) As a particular source of inspiration, he cited The Arabian Nights. Indeed, Unknown editor John W. Campbell, Jr., was soon to inform all in his stable "they aren't to do Arabian Nights because the field is preempted by L. Ron Hubbard." "Stamboul," circa 1939, speaks precisely of that world from which he drew so many now classic stories and novelettes.*

# STAMBOUL

(Featured on L. Ron Hubbard's The Joy of Creating album)

Deep in a forgotten desert
Leagues 'way from the crowded strand
Legends of long dead
Kingdoms
Lost in desert Sand
Legends of mighty nations
Minarets reaching to the sky
Now dust in the hands of Allah
Like the Kingdom of Stamboul

\* \* \*

Stamboul! Mightier than Baghdad
Ruled o'er by a godlike shah
Father of a dainty princess
Sweet girl they called Nazah
Toast of the desert chieftains
Coveted by a thousand men
Glory of the pride of Allah
The kingdom of Stamboul

\* \* \*

'Twas nearing Nazah's
sixteenth birthday
Suitors from every land
Merchants and dazzling
princes
Came seeking Nazah's
hand
Innocent, with eyes to
heaven
Wondering at the courtyard's
blare
Not knowing she was to
marry
For the glory of Stamboul

# A DEMON CAUGHT ME

 demon
Caught me
In my room
With a haunting
Yell
And a cry
Of doom
He leaped
And beat me
With a terror
Claw.

The threats
Of misery
And grave
The banishment of
Lord
To slave
The shriek
Of awfulness
And sin
He!

The howling ghastly fantasy
The awesome yowling
The horrid filthy travesty
of Gloom.

I quailed
And whined
For mercy I
Who had in heyday
Eight times slain the
Mightiest
of dragons
Me!

I whined and pled
And crawled abed
And begged
Yea begged for surcease
I!

A demon
Caught me in
My room
And I
Poor fool
Had fear enough
To weep.

## Bomber

*A renowned aviating pioneer through the early 1930s, Ron inevitably generated numerous stories and articles on the subject. Indeed, some of his first published works may be found within the pages of the air-enthusiasts' journal The Sportsman Pilot. Meanwhile, among his undergraduate fiction is the aforementioned Grounded.*

*In pursuit of story material, he writes of touring a Seattle, Washington, Boeing Aircraft plant "until I had bunions the size of onions." Nevertheless, results were memorable in the 1936 thrillers Test Pilot for Argosy and Sky Birds Dare! for Five-Novels Monthly. Then again, research at the Boeing plant also yielded "Bomber" as a sobering glimpse of what lay just five years away.*

# BOMBER

*Silver wings*
*Against*
*Blue sky*

*Diamond*
*Humming*
   *concrete fingers*
*Above the towers*

*Bellied in*
*Your womb*
*You carry*
*Death*
*To all this.*

## Suicide

*Almost immediately upon return from his 1932 Caribbean Motion Picture Expedition, Ron again set out for the southern latitudes—this time for Puerto Rico, where he headed that island's first complete mineralogical survey under United States protectorship.*

*He arrived by naval transport in early autumn to find himself in a classically adventurous world replete with gold-crazed prospectors, disreputable mining engineers and swindlers of all descriptions. Through various turns of his six-month trek, he ultimately hacked out jungle trails, crawled from collapsed mine shafts, wrestled with malaria and befriended an intensely spiritual jíbaro (native Puerto Rican). The classically tragic suicide—more or less glimpsed from afar amidst "a huddle of unpainted shacks"—was simply part of the larger tableau.*

*The details, recorded in a letter home, were as terse and etched as any from the island. A young American engineer forsakes his stateside fiancée for a local girl. After months of no word, and the marriage date long past, the jilted fiancée sets out on the engineer's trail. When she at last tracks him down, he withdraws to his shack, bolts the door and releases the safety on a service automatic. As Ron then so pointedly concluded, "The crash of a forty-five rips through the mountain air. The young engineer lies across his bed in a pool of blood, half his face shot away."*

*The poem inspired by this tragedy employs a dramatic first person in order to suggest we have stumbled upon the suicide note of that unfortunate mining engineer. It would seem to have been one of the earliest New York poems, possibly from 1935, when memories of that expedition were still fresh.*

# SUICIDE

*I knew*
*I wouldn't*
*But there I sat.*

*I knew*
*I wouldn't*
*But there I watched*

*Parading bottles*
*And*
*A gun.*

*I knew*
*I wouldn't*
*But here I had*
*In sweaty palm*
*A thing*
*called life.*

*It was some trinket*
*shivering there*
*While I*
*with cruel hard lips*
*And long tight fingers*
*Watched*
*And held*
*that thing.*

*I knew*
*I wouldn't*
*although*
*I knew*
*I could.*

# BORED

To sit
And listen
And
Pretend.

The subway is
a droning surf.

To read
And feel
That this
Is just a
Temporary ease
Soon lost.

To sit
And taste
this stale
Cigarette.

# CONDEMNED

No money in the streets
But only sweat
And
gutters.

I creep alone through crowds,
Jostled
Thrust aside....

As I look up I think
Of wide, free
places.

Oh there are trains
But I
Look up and see
Canyon walls with staring windows
Pressing in.
And know...

No money in the streets
But only
sweat
and gutters. *Ron*

# THE GARDEN

(Featured on L. Ron Hubbard's State of Mind album)

*These are the flowers*
*Which bloom for thee*
*In a secret place*
*'Twixt mind and soul*
*In a garden kept by*
*Me.*

*The laughter blooms—*
*The soft white petals*
*Of our tears—*
*The starry*
*Vivid blossoms of*
*Our ecstasy—*
*And giddy here*
*The reeling stems*
*All fashioned out from*
*Heady wines*
*And in the quiet place*
*Where none may view*
*the timid leaves*
*Of secrets kept—*

*Ah yes—*
*Each moment finds*
*Its counter here*
*Where air is sweet*
*And sped along*
*The purer*
*For the fragrance of*
*Our dreams.*

*These are the flowers*
*Which bloom for thee*
*In a secret place*
*'Twixt mind and soul*
*In a garden*
*Kept*
*By me.*

*Ah yes,*
*each moment finds*
*Its counter here*
*Where air is sweet*
*And sped along*
*The purer for*
*The fragrance of*
*Our dreams.*

# *The* EARLY BALLADS

# The
# Early Ballads

IN THE SUMMER OF 1940, AND AS PART OF THE GREATER research trail culminating in Dianetics and Scientology, Ron set out from Bremerton, Washington, bound for the Alaskan Panhandle. Dubbed the Alaskan Radio Experimental Expedition for the fact he sailed with a then novel radio navigation system, the voyage was partially sponsored by the United States Navy and conducted beneath an Explorers Club flag. Expeditionary aims included testing said navigation system, while simultaneously charting inland waterways and correcting coastal maps. This was also the voyage wherein Ron sought out North Coast Indian legends of a Great Flood not dissimilar to Biblical tales of Noah's Ark. In that respect, he was yet again seeking common denominators between diverse peoples and testing notions of racial memory.

Given the purely nautical achievement— some 1,500 miles of treacherous water in a 32-foot ketch—Ron's Ketchikan, Alaska, landing was no inconsiderable event. It immediately inspired newspaper headlines and "Voice of Alaska" radio KGBU summarily welcomed him onto the airwaves as a nautical commentator. (Inasmuch as L. Ron Hubbard was also, of course, an author of renown, he was further invited to host a local literary show-cum-new-talent-contest.) His particular slot was dubbed the "Mail Buoy" and featured Captain Hubbard responding to questions from listeners relating to seafaring matters: how best to rig a ketch or safeguard against shipboard fire. Yet to round out the hour, he also sang ballads—largely of his own composition and some reprinted here.

He was, as noted, a considerable balladeer— professionally performing while still attending university and possessing an admirable baritone. He was also an accomplished musician and the lyrics, of course, are self-evident. In the main, his topics were regional. "The Sofia," for example,

Expeditionary Captain L. Ron Hubbard in Ketchikan, Alaska, from whence he drew so many tales for his early nautical ballads

tells of an actual wreck with severe loss of life on Juneau's Vanderbilt Reef. Larry O'Connor was a Ketchikan personality of some notoriety—a self-styled poet in his own right and a Panhandle fisherman. Finally, and like many a wilderness outpost, Ketchikan boasted a "Waterfront Empress" and it inevitably proved the ruin of many a young man. ■

Thomas Basin, Ketchikan, Alaska: fisherfolk and roustabouts along the last American frontier; photograph by L. Ron Hubbard

## The Alaska Chief

*The signature ballad for Ron's Alaskan radio show, his recording of "The Alaska Chief," preceded every episode of the "Mail Buoy." The ballad itself tells of an all-too-typical disaster among the poorly maintained cannery fleets: an explosive mix of gasoline fumes and damp sparkplugs. Hence, Ron's warning to mariners: "A man might as well fish from a war-headed torpedo as from a fumy-bilged boat." As a further note on atmosphere, the piece was prefaced with this: "To be played at midnight on a Spanish guitar or ukulele with two jugs of whiskey—and with proper emphasis."*

# THE ALASKA CHIEF

*The Alaska Chief was a sturdy ship*
*With a burthen forty tons*
*She sailed the icy northern seas*
*To work the salmon runs.*

*She sailed the waves from Hecate Straits*
*To the north of Dundas Bay*
*And ever worked and never failed*
*Thruout the night and day.*

*The Alaska Chief was sixty feet*
*Her beam was just fourteen*
*She drew a fathom mark and two*
*And cut the water clean.*

*She worked the sea and stormy shore*
*Thru rip and tidal swell*
*Till came the day a gas tank leaked*
*Sad rang the Lutine bell.*

*The Alaska Chief was on the job*
*The first of the cannery fleet*
*To do the first of the season's work*
*And she was clean and sweet.*

*The sun was yet an hour from dawn*
*For the first of June was breaking*
*Her westing off the Dover shore*
*The Alaska Chief was making.*

Her crew of five with skipper brave
They saw the slow dawn making
They looked ahead to seamen's work
Nor thought of hearts soon breaking.

Far ashore in a little town
By name 'twas Ketchikan
Their wives looked fond on children sweet
As only mothers can.

They never knew when the cold dawn came
That brave men fought the wave
They could not know that even then
That five were drowned in an icy grave.

The gas tank boomed as the tide was turned
Away from the high tide mark
Four men went down to an icy grave
In the home of the squid and the shark.

No one knows how the gas tank flared
But we only know she sank
With never a skiff to carry them
And never a saving plank.

Delsman died when the ship went down
For he never reached the deck
He was the first of the gallant crew
To sink in that awful wreck.

The next to go was A. M. Accue
Fighting as a seaman can
He swam an hour in the icy sea
And drowned with the shore in scan.

He must have known that the bitter fight
Was against the ebbing tide
He surely knew but he never stopped
But swimming, sank and died.

Then Jack McQuire was the next to go
When brave heart stopped at last
He sank but he almost reached the shore
Thru the raging tide and blast.

The skipper brave had a heart of oak
And a body tried and true
He fought the tide and freezing cold
For an hour that past and two.

He reached the shore with broken strength
And grasped at the barnacled rock
He never knew for he fainted there
How the cold wind cut and mocked.

Jeered o'er the grave of his comrades four
Drowned in the icy sea
But the same sad fate that came to them
Still waits for you and me.

So sailors tall pause in your strength
To heed my sad grim warning
Lest you shall meet this same sad fate
Some gusty brawling (fatal) morning.

Be on your watch for gas boat fumes
'Tis the boatman's greatest bane
For hearts must break when the boat goes down
In the crash of blasting flame.

And those ashore shall feel no more
The joy of the boats in homing
For grey gull fly when the ship goes down
In the icy tidal, running.

## The Sofia

*The wreck of the SS Sofia is another tragic page in Alaskan maritime history. She was a coastal liner running the inside waterway between British Columbia and southeastern Alaska. Amidst blinding snow and gale-force winds, she ran aground on an infamous Vanderbilt Reef. As Ron's ballad suggests, her Captain was not initially alarmed and warned off rescue vessels until bad weather abated. The decision proved fatal and all passengers and crew perished.*

# THE SOFIA

O vanderbilt is a hidden reef
Just south of skagway town
Where low tide shows the fatal reef
Its fangs with seaweed brown.

'Twas there in a night of snow and Storm
In the year of sad sixteen
The Sofia sank and carried down
Three hundred and eighteen...

She strick the reef ere day had come
in the storm where the blizzard howled
she Struck and fast on the reef she ran
The wild sea leaped and growled.

Her skipper called her crew to him
And said, "My men, make ready
I do not think our ship will sink
for the tide is at its eddy."

Her bosun Stern has sailed the seas
for years a score or more
He said, "This ship is doomed sir,
Her hours are less than four."

Her Captain proud he laughed in glee
at the bosun's simple warning.
"The tugs are close and free we'll be
when comes tomorrow morning."

The bosun shook his head in doubt
and returned unto his duty.
"This sea is fanged with fire tonight
and gone is summer's beauty."

He thought of home at the Lion's Gate
In fair vancouver's harbor.
He thought of home and children dear
and his father's grape hung arbor.

He knew he'd see them nevermore
For the wind and the tide were swelling.
He knew he'd heard old Davy's crew
In a hundred Fathoms yelling.

The ice wind came from chilkat bay
and roared when the tide had turned
The shipman must have seen his fate
as his heart within him burned.

Her passengers they never knew
Of the death in the rising storm
They thought her decks were firm as steel
to keep them safe from harm.

The ship tore loose when the tide went out
in fathoms twenty-five
They went down deep to an icy grave
Not one was left alive.

The light still burns on sentinel isle
and the ice and the storm winds come
And crewmen watch for a blinking light
held on a tossing drum.

It marks the spot in an icy sea
And the grave of her hundreds dead
For many who sank are buried there
and the sea is their shroud and spread.

# THE ENGINEERS

*The engineer's a hardy man*
*Who toils amidst the smoke*
*He works with gas and diesel oil*
*That'd make an idol choke*

*He works and slaves from break of day*
*To make the engines run*
*And when the rest are fast asleep*
*His toilsome day is done*

*When the waves are rolling high*
*And the stormy seas go by*
*The engineer is down below*
*And smoke is in his eye*

*His knuckles bruised with broken tools*
*With wire and with curses*
*He makes the engine spit and run*
*And like a mother nurses*

*Rusted hunks of broken iron*
*And shattered bits of steel*
*The engineer's a handy man*
*His rust heap turns the wheel*

*For he's the daddy of them all*
*And while the boat's afloat*
*He keeps her running day and night*
*And is the skipper's goat*

*For many ships have sunk at sea*
*With engineers inside*
*He keeps his engine running true*
*For that's his simple pride*

He lives down in his dirty hell
Like a demon sunk in sin
He fights the heap with tool and claw
with wire and dollar gin

CHORUS
His hands are marked with honest toil
His fingernails with grime
The engineer's a hardy bloke
While he is in his prime

The skipper bold may stave the ship
Upon some well known rock
The engineer will pump her out
And plug her with a sock

He'll keep her dirty hulk afloat
And damn her deep to hell
But the engineer will do his job
And always do it well

L'ENVOI
Now Larry O'Connor, you big baboon
You claim to be a poet
Your rhymes are worse than I can tell
To read them is to know it
So here's a tune for the engineer
And I think that I've done it well
If you like my tune we'll have a drink
If you don't, just go to hell

## Waterfront Empress

*Decades after authoring his ballad of the "Waterfront Empress," Ron offered the following remembrance of his Ketchikan stay and it can hardly be improved upon:*

*"Everybody who gets in trouble with the state police and the Feds and everybody else will eventually turn up somewhere in the backwoods of Alaska—if they can make it.*

*"Nobody goes by his right name and they have a murder every morning for breakfast. It's not quite that bad because they're not murders, they're suicides. And they find a fellow with his head blown off by a shotgun—no sign of a shotgun, footprints all around, sound of tremendous struggle, the fellow's pockets emptied. The sheriff comes out, he takes a look at the body and he says, 'Huh! Suicide.'*

*"They have, there in Ketchikan, the only stream in the world where the fish and the fishermen go up to spawn—it's a red-light district. It stretches up around the curve of really a very beautiful little stream. But the buildings have trapdoors. Most of Ketchikan is built over water. The fishermen (it's mostly fishermen that come in there with any money) wear rather heavy rubber boots and water gets into these boots rather quickly and they go down rather fast.*

*"The air is in the boots at first and that holds the boots up till the fellow drowns and then the water fills and then the boots hold him on the ground. And then the tide there is rather fast and it sweeps the body out past Chacon, the cape there, and nobody ever knows anything more about it.*

*"But when the police do find a fisherman drowned or floating there in the straits, without anything in his pockets, they look him over very carefully and say, 'Hm! Suicide.'"*

*The very personification of a Ketchikan brothel, Ron's Waterfront Empress is the quintessential siren who lures wayward fishermen to their doom.*

# THE WATERFRONT EMPRESS

*The Waterfront Empress*
*And reigns by the Seine*
*With an air quite aplomb but*
*Demimondaine.*
*Her scepter's a bone*
*She stole off a dog*
*Her robe is a sack*
*Much too large*
*For a Hog*
*She issues her bulls*
*In a style vitriolic*
*And gobbles her fees*
*With a talon bucolic*
*She speaks in a bray*
*Not so cultured but loud*
*Which leaves her servitors*
*With eardrums quite*
*Plowed.*
*The lady has charm*
*In a violent way*
*Her mandates alarm*
*But bolster her sway*

*And if some dark nightly*
*you fall into her sphere*
*Speak to her gently*
*And buy her her beer*
*For she rather would hang you*
*Than sigh at your face*
*And probably bang you*
*With banished disgrace*
*The Waterfront Empress*
*And reigns by the Seine*
*With an air quite aplomb but*
*Demimondaine.*

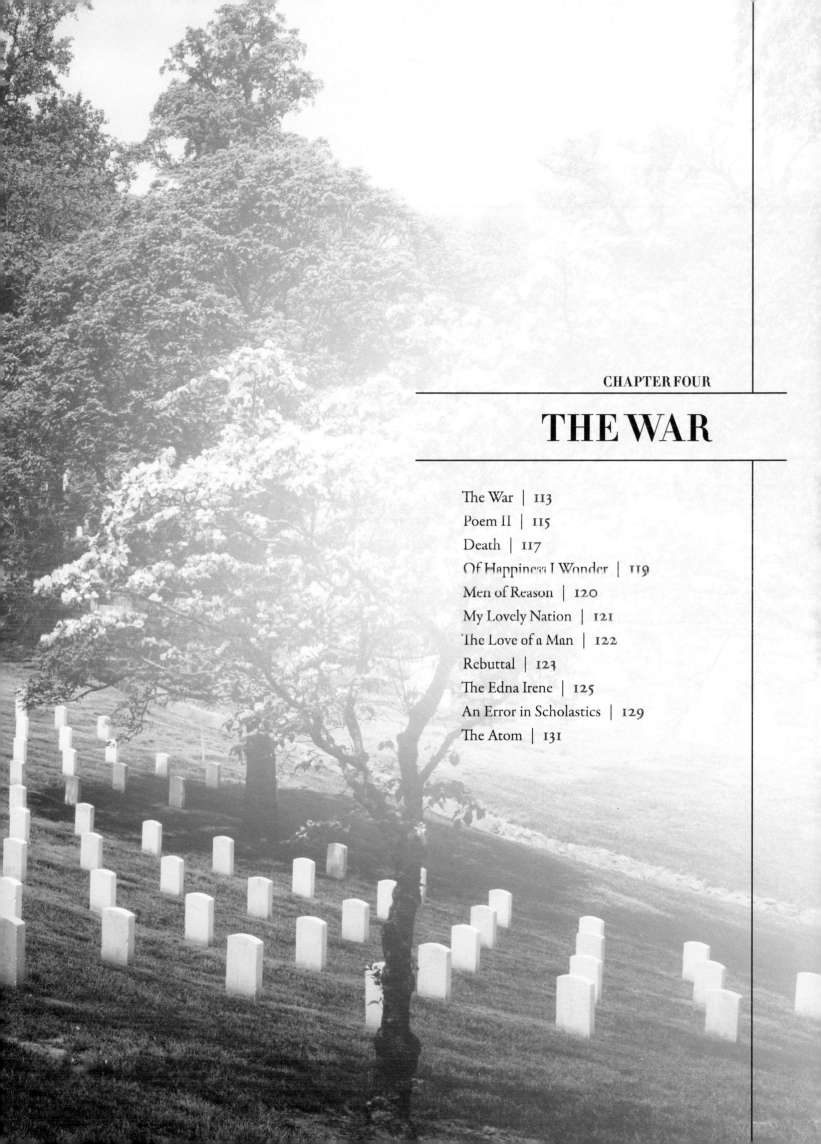

# THE WAR

# The War

HAVING ENTERED THE SECOND WORLD WAR AS A lieutenant (junior grade) in the United States Navy, L. Ron Hubbard spent the first months of 1942 as Senior Officer Present Ashore in Brisbane, Australia. His duties included counterintelligence and the organization of relief for beleaguered American forces on Bataan. It was in this latter capacity that he eventually saw action on the island of Java and only eluded capture through a daring escape on a raft. After fracturing an ankle in subsequent action, he was flown stateside (in the Secretary of the Navy's plane, no less) as the first American casualty returning from the Pacific Theater. After a short recuperative stint at the New York Cable Censor Office, he took command of an antisubmarine escort vessel with Atlantic convoys. Upon completion of seventy runs against enemy submarines, he received command of a submarine chaser in the Pacific, the sixty-man *PC-815*. It was aboard this vessel that he then engaged and destroyed two enemy submarines in action he would long regret:

"I, as a sailor, have sinned with the rest, it is true. On the bottom of the North Pacific there probably lie two 2,000-ton Japanese submarines, worth perchance a score of million dollars to the enemy before my depth charges sunk them. Perhaps not less than three hundred enemy lives struggled wetly out to Soldier Heaven. But it is better not to dwell upon these things. They should be dedicated to DUTY and recorded in files which are seldom opened. But the small voice cries (that inevitable small voice) and wonders if among them any could paint or appreciate the India ink sketches of a bamboo tree wherein the strokes must go as the tree must grow."

His poetry, written through equally reflective moments, expresses the same: "For no nation ever bought glory / With agony, death and burned towns." That much of it is bitter is appropriate, and all the more so when set at counterpoint to rhyme and predictable rhythms. Also included is a slightly later "The Atom" in grim contemplation of what the next war promised. ■

Lieutenant L. Ron Hubbard, 1944

# POEM II

The many lips which laughed with life
The many kisses that they gave
Are set in grim and deadly strife,
Are cut like cold stone, in the brave.
And lips that once have gaily sung
Are sad and silent bars.
And tears and blood from all are wrung
When lips pledge lives to wars.

Yet from sweaty ranks and muddy banks
Bursts forth a captive cry
And longing hearts at home give thanks
That voices cannot die
But live through change and time and space,
And through the centuries
For a peaceful, just, fraternal race
Utter impassioned pleas.

The many lips which laughed with life
The many kisses that they gave
Are set in grim and deadly strife,
Are cut like cold stone, in the brave.
But quiet lips, with unknown names,
Can make a mighty roar
When every pair of them proclaims
The sin and shames of war!

# DEATH

*Death
Hovers on muted wings,
While we
Wait breathlessly
And blind.*

# OF HAPPINESS I WONDER

*Of happiness I wonder*
*Whence come the saffron streams?*
*The bitterness and thunder*
*Are something less than dreams.*

*The echoes of the wailing*
*A race of tortured men*
*Of hope all unavailing*
*In sorrow's wretched glen.*

*Who taught the ugly lesson*
*That fear is rod to rule*
*That Might the drear obsession*
*Is life's most valued jewel?*

*Who sang the song sans merci*
*And eager made the flog*
*Made dance a thing subversive*
*And called man slave and dog?*

*Who canted hypocritic*
*Of good opposed to sin*
*Who founded on diseases*
*The Mores we drown in?*

*What of these lies*
*For good of race*
*To save our souls*
*With tong and mace?*

*Many a devil with steepled hands*
*Dwells in silk unpining*
*And many a goodly saintly man*
*Goes awfully short on dining.*

# MEN OF REASON

(Featured on L. Ron Hubbard's State of Mind album)

*The men of reason*
    *Nurtured light*
*To save a battered*
    *Earth—*

*The men of anger*
    *Scrambled high*
*To kill all things*
    *of worth*

*The men of anger*
    *Raged and fought*
*And out of anger*
    *Die*

*That spot of light*
    *Upon yon cliff*
*Has often guttered low—*

*But men of reason*
    *Try again——*

*A thousand eons*
*So.* Ron

# MY LOVELY NATION

*Who flatters you, my favored nation,*
*Flatters in vain.*
*When dreams are ruined*
*No flag or tinkling tongue can please the wound*
*Nor ease a people's pain.*

*Who boasts of you, my valiant nation,*
*Boasts blood and wrath.*
*While men die young*
*Faith falters, and ideals, once proudly sung,*
*In war's bleak aftermath.*

*Who lives for you, my lovely nation,*
*Hopes, and must wait;*
*Though your vain errors*
*Heap history with deep and terrible terrors,*
*We trust your final fate.*

# THE LOVE OF A MAN

(Featured on L. Ron Hubbard's The Joy of Creating album)

The love of a man's a delicate thing
Built of earthquakes
And thunder.
His pat is a bear paw
His kiss is a curse
His squeeze would burst
Granite asunder.
If all of his wooing
Were witnessed from off
And his jousts in life's list assembled
You'd think the debris
In his emphatic wake
The shambles of warfare resembled.
His woman she nags or
Spoils feast day with tears
And offers her softness
To blisters
while he buys her
New baubles
which no one can use
And scars her fair hide up
with whiskers.
The love of a man is a delicate thing
For the granite's but papier-mâché
His lady she dodges
And won't comprehend
That a soft love in man goes away!  *Ron*

# REBUTTAL

(FROM THE OAK KNOLL NAVAL HOSPITAL IN OAKLAND, CALIFORNIA, WHERE THEN
LIEUTENANT L. RON HUBBARD UNDERWENT TREATMENT FOR COMBAT WOUNDS IN 1945)

*The marquees of the paladins,*
*Defying sun with gold,*
*Ablaze with steel and guidon brave*
*Se faire valoir untold.*
*But how to dust this valiance*
*And dead chivalric Knight?*
*This modern "progress" can't be wrong*
*And Miniver Cheevy right!*

## The Edna Irene

*Having suffered severe injuries through the Second World War, 1946 found L. Ron Hubbard more or less recuperating on the California island of Santa Catalina. There he oversaw the administration of a local yacht club and, most important, continued upon the greater trail of research that would soon culminate in Dianetics: The Modern Science of Mental Health. In what amounted to a sideline, however, he also drafted an occasional piece for the Catalina Islander. "The Edna Irene," published anonymously, appeared in that newspaper on 21 November 1946.*

# THE EDNA IRENE

*A faithless friend on a gale-scarred day*
*Has let the "Edna Irene" go astray.*
*A parting line, a drifting moor*
*And a ship lies broken on Avalon Shore.*

*He said when he left, too ill to stand,*
*To the friend who steadied his quivering hand,*
*"Now well you know Nor'easters come*
*And my boat, though no considerable sum,*

*"Is all I own, by her I eat,*
*'By catching fish I buy my meat.*
*I fear to leave her here alone*
*For she is my all, my floating home.*

*"So promise me to treat her fair,*
*'For she's a friend that's in your care."*
*And so the friend, he smiled and swore*
*He'd surely tend the craft at moor.*

*Nor'easter came on Saturday,*
*And in the place where ripples play*
*Scythed white havoc of waves and din,*
*Screaming combers wild with wind,*

*And every ship not sailed away*
*Was smothered, tortured, by the spray*
*And vessels sawed at stubborn lines*
*Pitching, twisting masts and chines.*

Fearing the monstrous, bursting fight—
    Behind them Avalon beach fanged white—
The Edna Irene crept toward shore,
    Her line nigh parted—stricken sore!

In hospital bed her owner lay.
    The "friend" days past had gone away.
Then brave George Bibson breasted storm,
    Bribed to change a line not worn,

On a glittering, insured crystal toy
    Of no more use than kite to boy,
A yacht hard by the stricken boat,
    George passed Irene to sink or float.

The Edna Irene, like abandoned dead
    Shuddering back, the stones to wed
And striking thunder of surf and spray
    Crashed ashore in Avalon Bay.

Unwitting owner in hospital cot
    Heard of storm but worried not
For who would fail to trust a friend
    To the very day the world will end?

Lifted, pounded, twisted, crushed
    Over the ship the sea has rushed,
And surf and tide and wind held prey
    While Havoc reigned on Avalon Bay. *Ron*

## An Error in Scholastics

*Although Ron's elegy on bureaucratic barbarism speaks for itself, two notes of interest may be added to "An Error in Scholastics." In the first place, it is another from his recuperative stay on Southern California's Santa Catalina Island through 1946. In the second place, when decrying those who would slaughter their way to glory, he is foreshadowing the central plea of Dianetics: The Modern Science of Mental Health: "There is a higher goal, a better goal, a more glorious victory than gutted towns and radiation-burned dead. There is freedom and happiness and plenty and a whole Universe to be won."*

# AN ERROR IN SCHOLASTICS

*When a world lies steeped in ashes*
*And ground in Conquerors'*
*dust*
*And the screams of dreadful*
*dying*
*Fill the archives with blood*
*and lust*

*Then oh ye historians revel!*
*And trim your redoubtable*
*pen*
*And fill children's ears with*
*drivel*
*of patriots, heroes and*
*MEN.*

*Count Mankind's advances*
*in rapings*
*Chalk empire's rise by its*
*fall*
*And chatter of kings and*
*their apings*
*of virtues and chivalrous*
*all.*

*Bah! Feeble and outrageous*
*asses*
*What battle wrote any*
*but blood?*
*Fools, swim in inkpots and*
*squalors*
*And sing your great grandeurs*
*of mud.*

*For no nation ever bought*
*glory*
*With agony, death and*
*burned towns*
*And no king was ever*
*but gory*
*Who slaughtered his way*
*to renown.*

*Ye sing, damn your songs, of*
*the error*
*Ye transplant the dust to the*
*van*
*History never was story*
*That didn't crown Thinker the*
*Man.*

## The Atom

*Among the first to decry unrestrained nuclear buildup and testing, L. Ron Hubbard remains one of history's most potent voices for the sane management of atomic energy. His landmark series of lectures on radiation hysteria still stands as the definitive word on both what the atom bomb represents in terms of civilization's gravest threat and the ultimate answer to that threat. An early student of atomic energy, he was further the first to delineate precisely how the radioactive particle impacts upon the human cellular structure. With subsequent research through the 1950s, he pioneered the use of the B vitamin niacin as a catalytic for "running out" radiation exposure. This LRH discovery and others following from it have been used with enormous success by those exposed to excessive levels of radiation.*

*Written in the late 1940s, "The Atom," offers one of the sharpest condemnations of what he aptly dubbed an instrument of terror and societal control.*

# THE ATOM

About the embers of a lonely fire
    Three men pondered silently,
What problem theirs, do enquire:
    They answer all: The ATOM......

Once, mused he, the Philosopher....
    The ATOM was our servant,
And harnessed, tamed, this monster
    Know we all: The ATOM.......

Words in Rhyme, the Poet said,
    I wrote for all to listen;
But now, all Earth is dead;
    And with the ATOM smitten.

No savant I, nor poet yet,
    The Third stood cowed and humble;
Just a man who could not get
    An answer to: The ATOM!

Epilogue:

Their food is gone......
    They live not long......
And from the Earth,
    With no re-birth.......
Is stripped the Race of MAN.
    Yet remains all that CAN....... The ATOM......!

# PHILOSOPHIC VERSE

# Philosophic Verse

"WHAT IS GENERALLY MISSED," EXPLAINED L. RON Hubbard in reference to his life's greater course, "is that my writing financed research," and it was from that research that Dianetics and Scientology were born in the early 1950s. For three decades thereafter, his output of fiction fell to almost nothing—such were the demands of

further research and the administration of what soon became a truly worldwide movement. Now and again, however, and generally at the request of editors of Scientology publications, he managed a few lines of verse.

Strictly speaking, the poems of this period qualify as religious/philosophic and tend to reflect the central revelation of Scientology: Man is not his body, mind or any other corporal identity. Rather, he is an immortal spiritual being, possessing capabilities far in advance of those hitherto predicted. Hence, as proclaimed in "There Is No Compromise with Truth": "You are a spirit...full capable / of making space / and energy and time / and all things well." What

Scientology represents, then, is the route from existence as a human being who lives a life as one who, "walks and eats and dies," to a spiritual existence that even the most expressive verse may not adequately describe.

In that Scientology embraces the whole of our lives, the poems to follow are likewise expansive. The futility of a purely material existence, the consequences of a fear-based morality and the utter paradox of a spiritual being, "forgotten to yourself and hidden from the eyes of all..." Less literal, but no less expressive, are "From Sea of Dreams" and "I Have a Demonity" in celebration of the spirit as purely himself—unfettered, exterior and exuberantly creative. ■

A contemplative moment at
Medford Lakes, New Jersey, 1953

# FROM SEA OF DREAMS

(Featured on L. Ron Hubbard's The Joy of Creating album)

From Sea of Dreams
To Rainbow Gulf
He Danced
A Rigadoon
From Astro Bay
To Diamond Cliff
The Mountains of
The Moon
He balleted
And Curvetted
And Swept
A wide
Fandango
What graceful waste
in airless
Space
His fabulous
Tarango—
From here to
There and
There to
Here
In Waltzes un-
gravitic
He spun the whole of
Lunar Space in
Gyrates trog-
lodytic
Why, why this dance
of Astral
Plane
Sans audience or
Reason
Who, who this mad
Time footed lad
Such waste
of dance is
Treason.

## The Dianetic Jingles

*Dating from May of 1952, Ron's "Dianetic Jingles" were originally presented to students at the Hubbard College in Phoenix, Arizona, as a hastily mimeographed handout with no formal explanation. Merely, as Ron so insouciantly remarked: within these phrases exist "very broad" tenets of Dianetics therapy—if only one could dig them out. To which he added with characteristic modesty: "And please don't frame it."*

*The "Jingles" were later set to music and appear as "The Right Way to Be Is to Be" on L. Ron Hubbard's State of Mind album.*

# DIANETIC JINGLES

(Featured on L. Ron Hubbard's State of Mind album as "The Right Way to Be Is to Be")

*Anything you can take, you can make.*

*Anything you can see, you can be.*

*Anything you shun will have won.*

*Anything you have done, you can do.*

*Anything that is work is a shirk.*

*Anything you desire means expire.*

*If you ever need bait, just create.*

*If a motion comes in, use and win.*

*If a motion you won't use, you will lose.*

*If all motion comes in, that's a sin.*

*If motion from you flows, the world glows.*

*If beauty you desire, beauty transpire.*

*If tone tends toward spin, you're taking motion in.*

*If tone is to soar, create even more.*

If you don't want the real, always steal.

If you want the whole sky, never buy.

If you don't want remorse, just be source.

If you don't want to see, with all motion agree.

If you want to be tall, just be all.

If you ever repent, you are spent.

If you act in today, you keep morrow away.

If you act in the past, you won't last.

If you have to be liked, you are spiked.

If you choose to agree, you're a tree.

If you want others' gain, you're insane.

If all things you eschew, they are glue.

If your body you'd leave, don't believe.

The way out of MEST ain't detest.

If you'd soar to the blue, just go through.

If all things you would flee, these you'll be.

If you want to destroy, just annoy.

If you just want to heal, make him real.

All the things that come in are a sin.

Whatever is cause, to it everything draws.

Whatever is wrecked was effect.

If high tones shun the low, the suns brighter glow.

When a high tone fights entheta, he comes in very later.

Entheta is just matter kicking up a final splatter.

If your MEST is in disorder, your case is on the border.

If your MEST is in good shape, you haven't time to hate.

If all things you would create, you'd better be in time and date.

If through other's thoughts you plow, you will come at last to Now.

If you don't want to be attacked, don't draw back.

If all evil you'd burn down, simply up and build a town.

There is no trick to being, unless you spend your time agreeing.

If you don't have a datum, create 'em.

The only unknown are in other men's domes.

The real universe is a hearse.

The right way to be is to be.

When aesthetics are sex, there've been wrecks.

*If you want to be pure, don't endure.*

*If you want to last, just move fast.*

*If all things you'd deserve, don't preserve.*

*If the world's all your brother, you're just another.*

*Those who gave us mystic were sadistic.*

*No wise man should stammer because another shuns his grammar.*

*Don't ever go downscale because* MEST *won't get up and cheer and hail!*

*If you would overrate, just let it make you wait.*

*The bottom of disease is anxiety to please.*

*You can blame your whole confusion on the fact you bought illusion.*

*The always last-sung song—"I was wrong."*

*You'll never climb a steeple if you worry about people.*

*If all misery is bested, you've the universe invested.*

*Just because it made you fall doesn't prove that it is all.*

*If you get caught in the middle, it's because you've bought a riddle.*

*If you want things in delirium, just get serium.*

*If the engrams you'd keep in, study hard to know of sin.*

*If you want an empty larder, tell yourself you must work harder.*

If your vision is all blurry, you've bought another's worry.

If you want to be in chains, let some other buy your brains.

If from another's grace you'd fall, just pretend that you aren't all.

If you find yourself well under, it's because you defined blunder.

The entire source of pain is an effort to abstain.

A calm and peaceful mind has refused to put trouble behind.

A really sharp obsession is from lack of self-confession.

If you want to really let it, forget it.

If you want to get real tragic, forget it was just magic.

If you really want the stutters, respect the rights of others.

If you want to be tearful, be careful.

The upset of tradition is the way to eat roast pigeon.

The craving for a drink is creation of a brink.

The desire to be hugged is a craving to be drugged.

A creeping inhibition is a stable definition.

The only reason some people find ambition is a spike, is they don't try to be, they try to be **like**.

If you're awfully deject, you're defect.

## Demonity

*One afternoon in early 1955, while attending to administrative duties in his office at the Scientology center in Phoenix, Arizona, Ron was approached by the editor of Scientology's Ability magazine and asked to supply a poem. A reasonably accomplished poet himself (and erstwhile friend of none other than Ezra Pound), the editor had long intended to include scraps of verse in the journal. In reply, we are told of Ron pausing for a reflective moment or two, "then jotting down five decisive lines that seemed to say a lot about the man, because they were honest and spontaneous."*

## AN ODE TO CIRCUITS

*I*have a deity
It sits
Upon a mist
And says
Nuts. *ℓ~*

## I HAVE A DEMONITY

*I*have a demonity
It spins
Amongst the bins
And says
? *ℓ~*

# LOST

*Lost to the brightness of morning*
*Stopped short of sunset's cool glow*
*Battered and twisted and missing*
*In the doom where the lost storms go*

*Not known were the laws of the Holy*
*Confused were the courses thou ran*
*Tangled in webs of thy making*
*Failed because thy name is Man*

# STONE AGE RELIGION

*On a delicate*
*diet of virgin*

*The Image*
*resplendently*
*dined*

*With ogle eyes*
*smiling like*
*sturgeon*

*And populace*
*kindly inclined*

## Eulogy for a Friend

*In 1957, upon the passing of South African entertainer and L. Ron Hubbard's longtime friend, Peggy Conway, Ron penned this eulogy. Given what Scientology reveals as regards our immortality, "From body's birth to / Body's grave and then / To birth again," as the Scientology funeral service reads, his close is apt: "Then let Death die!"*

# EULOGY FOR A FRIEND

*D*eath becks
and whispers slyly
In our ears
"Come
"Lie down
"And softly
"Sleep."

So easy now this slumber
Deep
So quiet now the
Pressures of
A life.

"Come Sleep"
Says death
"And give up strife and striving
"And lie down.

"Then nevermore
"The tiredness to weep
"Not once again."

Ah death what treachery
thou hast
To lie so softly to
Our weariness.
For hell itself is gained
By giving up.

Each backward step
But takes us nearer to
A brink
Of Fierce Endure
And each back pace
        we make
Is but a stride we'll
        have to take
'Gainst the tide again.

How glib
How easy now to purr
"Death is but sleep
"Lie down and rise no
        more."

For death and sleep alike
But slide us down a grade
That we
Must climb if we
Would then be free.

What humor it must be
        to Death
When we
find out we have
        but lost
Another mile
We must
Make back
And when we find
From off the bier
the weariness of
        a life
Unrecompensed
With friends or what
We learned the last.

Death
Solves nothing
But our joy.

"Give up!"
Thus speak the traitors of
Our lives.
"Grow tired, old and
"Die!

"And be no menace to us
"Now whose life
"You threaten with
"Your breath."

A placid far
And unreached day
'Twould be when I
laid back and let
The song of death
'Bequeath me tortured
miles I must face up again.

I live.
And Death?
Then let Death die!

## A Funeral Oration for Homo Sapiens

*With his "Funeral Oration for Homo Sapiens," Ron is invoking an old and memorable poetic form: the oratorical lament for a fallen hero. Among other notable examples: Pericles' eulogy to the Peloponnesian dead, Antony's farewell to Caesar and the Gettysburg Address. That Ron further eulogizes a bomb-pitted Earth is all the more ironic. The poem originally appeared in Scientology's Ability magazine and dates from the summer of 1957 or at the height of US-Soviet nuclear posturing.*

# A FUNERAL ORATION
# FOR HOMO SAPIENS

From treetop stepped
Into
The Bravery of Cave
Who feared you, Man?
The animals that
Fattened on your Child?
Not they?
The lice that ate your armpits
and your pelf?
Not they?
Big toothed Man
Whose teeth
Would scarcely scratch
A fang,
Who feared you then?
Not they, the animals of Earth.

But eons later, Man,
You showed them sure.
For there they lie
The species that once sneered.
They're dead
The pigeon and the fawn, the otter and the swan,
You showed them, Man.
With fire, plunder and the
Sword
You showed them, Man,
And now they're dead
Sorry
Doubtless
That they sneered.

And you,
Grown big in weapons
Small in sense,
Where are you, Man?
Under the clouds
of H-Bomb pitted Earth
You sleep.
Where are you now, O Man?

And they, the ones you showed
In your brief bow
Into Eternity,
They sleep.
Ah, peaceful now the Earth
With none to mourn
or Sigh
For your demise.
How Quiet here,
This grave called
Earth.

But doubtless you
        knew best.
You showed them sure.
Unfortunate it is
You showed yourself
As well.
Was it worth it, Man?
Amen.

## There Is No Compromise with Truth

*With the founding of Scientology in 1952 came several definitive LRH statements as to what this new religious philosophy represented vis-à-vis his discovery of Man as "the immortal, imperishable self, forevermore." These statements are contained in his books, articles and tape-recorded lectures. For yet another kind of statement on the matter, however, there is "There Is No Compromise with Truth" from June 1961.*

# THERE IS NO COMPROMISE
# WITH TRUTH

*There are those*
*who would have me compromise with truth and tell you other things,*
*for greed and popularity*
*For lies might then resound*
*my name*
*and theirs into*
*some future state of granite and concrete.*

*But then*
*there is no war not based on lies,*
*there is no infamy alive without*
*its kindred kin, deceit.*

*For I care nothing, yes and less*
*for fame*
*or for the crowd*
*whose howls are music to a fool*
*but din*
*to me*

*Truth*
*alone can echo far and as it springs*
*from spirit so*
*alone can outlive clay.*
*And if in speaking as a spirit men*
*forget as men most often do*
*my name*
*then it is naught*
*to me.*
*For there is truth in that*
*a name to live*
*must speak*
*in riddles or in lies.*

*The want of belly*
*and of eye*
*of one mere transient man*
*cannot*
*be weighed to outweigh more*
*than Truth.*

*So truth I speak*
*and know*
*for long that jest*
*and misery await*
*the one who dares*
*and forget self*
*and say*
*no compromise with fact—*
*since fact*
*erases self*
*and more and is*
*the magic sign*
*which brings*
*the Universe to naught.*

*For wealth can live alone*
*by mirroring a lie*
*and thus it is*
*with all things thick*
*and wide.*
*You are a spirit, then,*
*you Man, and not a Man*
*at all.*
*You are a spirit and you dwell*
*within the guts of mortal beast.*

*You have been eaten and your dreams,*
*and you*
*that cannot perish have*
*beguiled yourself*
*to perish with*
*the thought*
*that perish then you do.*

*You are a Spirit, then*
*a god,*
*full capable*
*of making Space*
*and energy and time*
*and all things well.*
*And there you crouch, forgotten*
*to yourself and hidden from*
*the eyes of all*
*pretending there to be*
*a beast*
*that walks and eats and dies.*

*You are a Man?*
*Then what*
*is Man,*
*this paradox*
*that baffles even he?*
*He is a beast*
*that walks upright*
*and thinks*
*he thinks—*
*but then this is not all.*
*He is a Spirit*
*guiding to a beast,*
*who sees the way*
*before*
*the legs*
*and leads*
*to higher peaks of*
*honor and of*
*love.*
*For think you that a beast can give*
*his word*
*or love much else*
*than belly and to breed?*

*Who are you, Man,*
*when we,*
*with all our*
*skills do extricate*
*you*
*from*
*that flesh?*
*Tell us is*
*that body*
*Joe, Mary,*
*Mae or Bob?*
*Does it then answer while*
*it breathes?*
*Or does the Spirit, flying near*
*look down*
*and use*
*that mouth and name?*

*When we of Scientology*
*have brought*
*you*
*from that flesh while it still lives,*
*then which is Joe?*
*The Spirit or*
*the flesh?*

*The body is a beast which moves*
*and has*
*a name,*
*a thing which dies*
*when asked to live upon*
*itself*
*as any Spirit could.*
*This complex miracle*
*the flesh*
*is made to be*
*compelling **and** complex—*
*for how else could it keep a soul*
*than by its tricks*
*and ills,*
*fatigues and whimperings?*

*You,*
*you are the spirit—*
*you,*
*you have*
*no extra soul—*
*you,*
*YOU are the soul—*
*if dulled too well*
*with flesh.*

*They come, these lords, Messiahs all*
*and say*
*this Truth and then*
*some Man with soul interned*
*perverts*
*their words*
*and gives*
*you half a truth.*
*They come, these Krishnas and these Christs*
*and say*
*to you their truth*
*and while their footsteps*
*stay, not yet blown out*
*in desert sand,*
*some fool with half a mind and greed for his own name*
*will give you half a truth.*

They say to face a fact as fact—
They tell you where
you err— They say
there is no force
yet made that can be stayed
with force—that
only
if
you
face
it
as
it
is
and change
it
not
at
all
will
you
be
free. And yet
before they've gone some echo
of them speaks
a part such as
to "turn the other cheek."

They say
you must take good
with bad and only then
be free
and others
say they said repent
and seek then to enslave a Man who
truly
is a soul.
They
in all ten thousand years
have told you truth
and echoes
have said half
and so
we find you here, a soul
in man
never
to be free?

But I
who am no sage, no name,
no message come
with mighty horns or runners in
the van—
I
who am no more than you
can say—
Face not half facts but all—
you can be free!
You are a soul. And not a Man.
The sky
awaits.

# *The* LATER SONGS

# The
# Later Songs

I N ADDITION TO BALLADS FROM HIS ALASKAN SOJOURN OF
1940, there remains a substantial body of L. Ron Hubbard lyrics
from the mid-1970s and early 1980s. These lyrics are reflective of a considerable
musical output and particularly so through the later decades of his life. In fact,
quite apart from his "soundtracks" to *Battlefield Earth* and *Mission Earth,* Ron

organized and composed for various musical groups. He also scored numerous Scientology films and, of course, wrote all songs appearing on his Scientology album, *The Road to Freedom.* Lyrics from these various and sundry works are as diverse as the musical styles he mined.

The earliest of these lyrics date from Ron's days aboard the research vessel *Apollo,* his home from 1969 to 1975. Long an aspect of shipboard life, music became a definite pursuit with his formation of the Apollo Troupe in 1974 as a gesture of goodwill and cultural exchange. The *Apollo* songs reprinted here are typical of his work from these years—free spirited and exuberant.

Lyrics from the 1982 *Battlefield Earth* album, aptly entitled *Space Jazz,* represent yet another direction entirely. The first-ever soundtrack to a novel, the album recounts, in song, the epic tale of Jonnie Goodboy Tyler's struggle to free

Mankind from alien Psychlos and then restore world peace. The album is especially notable for its employment of the Fairlight Computer Musical Instrument (CMI). Then largely unexplored, the CMI represented not a new form of synthesizer to *replicate* sounds, but the first means of digitally recording or *sampling* a sound and then presenting it through a keyboard as notes. To cite but one memorable example from *Space Jazz* itself: while the plaintive cry of wolves becomes a blues melody, the blast of guns becomes the rhythm. That L. Ron Hubbard was factually the first to realize the potential of the CMI becomes yet another fascinating footnote of his life.

No less innovative are the songs from Ron's ten-volume magnum opus, the *Mission Earth* series. One of the grandest satires of modern fiction, the series also stands as one of the most

The Poet/Lyricist in the south of France, 1968

successful, with all ten volumes successively rising to international bestseller lists. The canvas is as vast as all human folly and the author's foil as keen as they come. Among other significant issues addressed is the wholesale rape of natural resources, unrestrained pollution in the name of corporate profit, the erosion of morality and the willful proliferation of drugs in the name of societal control. The author is not, however, bitter. He is gentle, urbane and smiling—all underscored by the hundreds of lyrics and poems scattered through the text.

From the latter songs of L. Ron Hubbard come selections off Ron's Scientology musical statement, *The Road to Freedom*. Essentially religious music in Scientology style, *The Road to Freedom* offers ten LRH compositions to convey fundamental Scientology truths: that there is more to life than our purely physical existence, that our happiness and well-being lie entirely within us, that we can, indeed, achieve our dreams and, most significantly, that the death of our body is meaningless in view of our greater immortality.

Not included for the fact it stands at more than a thousand lines, but certainly bearing mention, is L. Ron Hubbard's *Hymn of Asia*. An epic poem reflecting his long-biding concern for those whom he described as spiritual cousins to Scientologists, *Hymn of Asia* comprises a deeply personal message to Eastern people and an affirmation of the human spirit. The entirety of the work was subsequently put to music and the full text is now available with compact disc.

Finally, and similarly celebrating the intrinsic power of the human spirit, are the lyrics inspiring *State of Mind* and *The Joy of Creating*. As the titles suggest, here are songs that would seem to comprise a summation of all L. Ron Hubbard had to offer as an artist and a man. ∎

Make It Go Right

The Way to Happiness

The Road to Freedom

The good go free

Laugh a Little

...ck you for listening

# WHAT I WANT IS HAPPINESS

(Featured on L. Ron Hubbard's State of Mind album)

What I want is
    Happiness
Hate and strife just
    bring sadness

The World may be an
    awful mess
But what I want is
    Happiness

Life is not
Captivity
There is an end
to Slavery

Men grow old
But I go free.
Why not try
To be like me?

The night is very
    cold and dark
But here there is
    a vital spark

My soul is like a
    lonely star
Diamond sparkling
    from afar

Love is ALL
LIFE MEANS TO ME
When Love is gone
Please Set me Free

Men grow old
But I go free
Why not try to
Be like me?

I was once as
  sad as you
Had my earthly
  Troubles too

Then I earned vitality
In Finding Scientology

To Say Goodbye
IS NOT TOO HARD
WHEN ONE'S LOVE
WITH HATE IS MARRED

Men grow old
But I go free
Why not try
To be like me?

What I want is
  Happiness
Hate and strife just
  bring sadness

The World may be an
  awful mess
But what I want is
  Happiness

BLACK AND GLOOM
WITHOUT A SMILE
MAKES OUR LIVING
NOT WORTHWHILE

Men grow old
But I go free
Why not try
To be like me?

## I'm Happy & Easy Livin'

*Although his lyrics from the Apollo years stand nicely alone, it might be noted that accompanying music for "I'm Happy" was drawn from a traditionally joyous Mideastern harvest song, "El Ameh," while "Easy Livin'" employed distinctly Oriental strains.*

# I'M HAPPY

(Featured on L. Ron Hubbard's State of Mind album)

Oh I'm Happy I'm Happy
    I'm Singing
  I'm singing I'm singing
    Today

  The world is smiling it's smiling
    And friendly
  And the best luck is on
    its way

  I know I'll make it
    this time
  And all the world
    will be mine
  And no one
    Can say No!

When I awoke in
    the dawn
I saw the clouds
    were all gone

I said this is
    the day
I'll have
    my way

Then the sky was
    all blue
With the Sun
    shining too
And I really
    could say
That this was my day

*They'll roll the red carpet*
  *Right up to my door*
*And rose petals and diamonds*
  *To cover the floor*

*They've opened all*
  *doors*
*That once barred*
  *the way*
*They'll paint all the*
  *skies with*
*"This is her day"*

*Oh I'm Happy I'm Happy*
  *I'm Singing*
*I'm singing I'm singing*
  *Today*

*The world is smiling it's smiling*
  *And friendly*
*And the best luck is on*
  *its way*

*I know I'll make it*
  *this time*
*And all the world*
  *will be mine*
*And no one*
  *Can say No!*

# EASY LIVIN'

(FEATURED ON L. RON HUBBARD'S STATE OF MIND ALBUM)

*Easy Livin'*
*Grass and Sunshine*
*Sparkling water*
*Sighing Trees*

*Birds are playing*
*Life is lovely*
*I will find it*
*Some Sweet Day*

*Easy Livin'*
*Lying Lazy*
*Need no money*
*None to Worry*

*I may be hoping*
*Not just dreaming*
*I will Find It*
*Some Sweet Day*

# FUNERAL FOR A PLANET

(FEATURED ON L. RON HUBBARD'S SPACE JAZZ ALBUM)

What planet is that?

I don't know, God.

Why, it's dead!

I hear a woman weeping.

Let's go closer.

The dead were not mourned.
Nobody cried,
Only trees wept.

Poor Earth.

A lonely wind sighed,
A planet had died
Not even a tomb.

Poor Earth.

Struck with pure hate
The warning too late
Gutted and raped.

Poor Earth.

Who will defend her?
Who will then mend her?
Who will befriend her?

Poor Earth.

Poor Earth.

Poor Earth.

That's not a woman crying.

That's the planet.

## Declaration of Peace

*Reflective of a lifelong commitment to world peace, lyrics from Space Jazz's "Declaration of Peace" were reprinted on thousands of parchments and bestowed on Ron's behalf to those organizations dedicated to the same ends.*

# DECLARATION OF PEACE

(Featured on L. Ron Hubbard's Space Jazz album)

*H*EAR ME!!

*Out of a hell
of shot and
shell,*

*Out of this
chaos of
contention,*

*Let us bring
peace to
pointless
fight.*

*Why do we court
the whore
called war?*

*Why make of
Earth a
shattered night?*

*There is no
ecstasy
in killing.*

*Love alone
can make
man
willing.*

*So hear me
warriors,
hear me
mothers.*

*There is no
pay in
slaughtered
brothers.*

*Attention, if
your sense
is fair,
heed that which
we now
declare.*

*PEACE! You
races far
and wide.
Peace!
Abandon your
blood-soaked
suicide
and now
abide
in peace!*

*Echo me!
As in your
hearts
you yearn for
love, not
death!*

*PEACE, we
have
declared it.*

*Snarls and strife
must be at end!
In peace alone
can this Earth mend.*

*And now find
ecstasy in
love,
love for Earth,
for all.*

*The gods of
peace have
now spoken.*

*OBEY!*

## Treacherous Love &
## Marching Song of the Protesters

*Although satirically treated through the pages of Mission Earth, rampant drug abuse and environmental pollution were, in truth, of deep concern to L. Ron Hubbard. (In testament to that fact are the nearly twenty years he devoted to the development of an effective drug rehabilitation program and the means to rid the human body of environmental toxins.) In a lyrical expression of that concern stands "Treacherous Love" and "Marching Song of the Protesters." The first, a wry description of opiate allure is self-explanatory. To "Marching Song of the Protesters," it should be added that Edgar Winter's recording of the song was later adopted as a marching anthem for the twentieth anniversary of Earth Day International, and proceeds from the single went to the United Nations environmental cause.*

# TREACHEROUS LOVE
# (OR WOOING THE POPPY)

(Featured on L. Ron Hubbard's Mission Earth album)

*My friends told me you were deadly,*
*I did not believe them then.*
*The blushing bloom upon your cheeks,*
*Lured and pulled me in.*

*Coy you were and hard to get,*
*Eluding my embrace.*
*But promises, oh promises,*
*And then at last a taste.*

*I wound myself about you.*
*Each kiss I took begged more.*
*I felt myself a mountain tall,*
*In heaven I would soar.*

*And then at last you'd given me*
*A glut of deadly sin*
*No matter what I took of you*
*It could not fill me in.*

*And then at last there I writhed*
*Tortured and convulsed*
*Fever soaring unassuaged*
*By friends and all repulsed.*

*I lay in ghastly agony*
*All joy in life had passed*
*And you, you whore, you,*
*You just stood there and laughed.*

# MARCHING SONG OF THE PROTESTERS (CRY OUT)

(Featured on L. Ron Hubbard's Mission Earth album)

Once it was a very nice planet
A home for those of us who care
But there are fools in high places
Who foul the sea and air
They dump the land with toxic waste
They spill the sea with oil
They poison plant and animal
And irradiate the air and soil

Chorus:
We've got to, Cry out, Protest
Object, Be heard
Day in, day out
This fight must never rest
It's time to save the world
Cry out, Protest
Object, Be heard
Let's raise a shout
Make this our common quest
To build a better world

And that's not the worst,
The deadly burst of radiation fission looms
Threatening to send the lot of us
To our collective dooms
To hell with those whose carelessness
In pollution is expressed
To hell with force politics
Where victory is only death

Chorus

This planet once was so alive
And nature bloomed in every spot
The time to save the Earth is now
'Cause it's the only home we've got

Chorus *Ron*

# LAUGH A LITTLE

(Featured on L. Ron Hubbard's The Road to Freedom album)

*When the world seems down on you*
*And grey clouds hide the sun,*
*When tears and rain commingle*
*And life's no longer fun*

*Laugh a little*
*Laugh a little*
*Ha ha, ha ha*
*Ha ha, ha ha*

*When all the world around you*
*Is deep enmeshed in frowns*
*When mother, sister, aunt and wife*
*All seem to have the downs*

*Laugh a little*
*Laugh a little*
*Ha ha, ha ha*
*Ha ha, ha ha*

*No need to weep or rant or rave*
*Or grind your teeth or shout*
*For if you laugh why then you'll soon*
*Find something to laugh about.*

*Ha ha ha ha,*
*Ha ha ha ha*

# THE GOOD GO FREE

(Featured on L. Ron Hubbard's The Road to Freedom album)

Try to live a decent life
Of truth and honesty
And you will find
With a peaceful mind
The good go free.

Chorus:
The good go free
The good go free

Be polite to your fellows
Be tolerant of the weak
And understand
That a hostile hand
Will rarely make them meek.

Avoid temptations of the flesh
For vices are a trap
And put you in
A coil of sin
Whose tentacles will enwrap.

Chorus

Fun is not found in wickedness
But in creativity
And you can court
Your favorite sport
Or pleasant industry.

Forgo all plans of vengeance
As hate was forged in Hell
And will stick you
With bitter glue
To whomever you would quell.

Don't agree with evil
Stand aside when it is planned
For an evil deed
Recoils with speed
And grips like chain and brand.

Reach outward to create your life
Produce what must be done
And be stern-willed
And very skilled
And shabby counsel shun.

CHORUS

When you wake each morning
Be sure to plan your day
To only do
Good things all through
And from that do not stray.

Try to live a decent life
Of truth and honesty
And you will find
With a peaceful mind
The good go free.

CHORUS

# THE WAY TO HAPPINESS

(Featured on L. Ron Hubbard's The Road to Freedom album)

*It takes skilled living to survive*
*For the road of life is rough.*
*And moral fiber, not brute force*
*Is the thing which makes one tough.*

*But what are the things called morals*
*We're told we must not sin*
*And warned that we must not trespass*
*But seldom once wherein.*

*So true, so true.*
*The way to happiness, it's the way to happiness*
*So true, so true.*
*The way to happiness, it's the way to happiness.*

*In a slack society,*
*Proceeding to decay,*
*It can even become an amusing thing*
*To casually steal and slay.*

*But must one do as one's fellows*
*And go the route to gloom*
*And say, it doesn't matter*
*If the world becomes a tomb?*

*There is a way to happiness*
*Whatever the rest may say.*
*It takes the bumps out of the road*
*And even paves the way.*

*If you'd attain survival*
*There are certain vital rules*
*That light the darkest highway*
*With lights that shine like jewels.*

*That is the road to happiness*
*A moral road it's true*
*And happiness and survival*
*Are partners with virtue.*

*So take the road to happiness*
*It's offered without fee*
*And survive my friend, in happiness*
*As a favor just to me.*

# A Final Work

"Capturing my own dreams in words, paint or music and then seeing them live," wrote a young L. Ron Hubbard, "is the highest kind of excitement." Nor would that excitement ever dim, and therein lay the spirit behind all LRH creativity—whether film, music, photography, prose, verse or lyrics. In that same spirit, and comprising the final selection from *The Road to Freedom* is "Thank You for Listening." It features a rare a cappella recording of what Ron described as his musical L'Envoi, i.e., his concluding stanza in dedication to listeners. Posthumously discovered on a demonstration cassette, the song was remixed and placed to music to serve as the album's closing selection. Given what these lyrics express, however, "Thank You for Listening" would also seem to serve as a fitting L'Envoi for all he presented as a poet and lyricist. ■

Yet another poetic perspective from Ron's home in southern England; photograph by L. Ron Hubbard, 1964

# *L'Envoi*
# Thank You for Listening

*Thank you for listening*

*I write just for you*

*But others hearing this may find*

*Things they would argue.*

*I do not sing what I believe*

*I only give them fact*

*If they believe quite otherwise,*

*It still will have impact.*

*For truth is truth and if they then*

*Decide to live with lies*

*That's their concern, not mine my friend,*

*They're free to fantasize.*

L. RON HUBBARD

# APPENDIX

# DISCOGRAPHY

*Listing of L. Ron Hubbard Album Songs*

## Album: Space Jazz
(SOUNDTRACK FOR BATTLEFIELD EARTH)

Golden Era of Sci Fi

Funeral for a Planet

March of the Psychlos

Terl, The Security Director

Jonnie

Windsplitter

The Mining Song

The Drone

Mankind Unites

Alien Visitors Attack

The Banker

Declaration of Peace

Earth, My Beautiful Home

## Album: Mission Earth
(SOUNDTRACK FOR MISSION EARTH)

Mission Earth

Treacherous Love

Bang-Bang

Teach Me

Cry Out (Marching Song of the Protesters)

Just a Kid

The Spacer's Lot

Joy City

# Album: The Road to Freedom
(Scientology songs)

The Road to Freedom

The Way to Happiness

The Worried Being

The Evil Purpose

Laugh a Little

The Good Go Free

Why Worship Death?

Make It Go Right

The ARC Song

L'Envoi, Thank You for Listening

# Album: Hymn of Asia
(The oratorio of L. Ron Hubbard's epic for the East)

Hymn of Asia

## Album: State of Mind
(A MUSICAL ADAPTATION OF L. RON HUBBARD'S VERSE AND SONG)

Men of Reason

Easy Livin'

What I Want Is Happiness

The Garden

The Castaway Song

Drum, Drummer

State of Mind

I'm Happy

A Clever Man

Above It All

The Right Way to Be (Is to Be)

## Album: The Joy of Creating
(A MUSICAL ADAPTATION OF L. RON HUBBARD'S VERSE AND SONG)

The Joy of Creating

Theta, Theta, See You Later

From Sea of Dreams

The Love of a Man

We're Going Up While the World Goes Down

The Sum of Man

Blue Endless Sea

Stamboul

Song of the Bard

Envoi

# ALPHABETICAL

*Listing of L. Ron Hubbard Poems*

# GLOSSARY

**abed:** in bed. Page 81.

**a cappella:** (of a song) sung without instrumental accompaniment. Page 191.

**acerbic:** harsh or severe in temper or expression. Page 58.

**aesthetic:** something that is artistically pleasing or beautiful; also, relating to the beautiful as distinguished from the merely nice, the useful, etc. Page 2.

**affirmation:** the action of *affirming*, stating positively or with confidence; declaring to be true. Page 168.

**aft:** toward the rear of a ship. Page 23.

**air-enthusiast:** of or for people who are filled with enthusiasm for flying and other topics in the field of aviation. Page 82.

**airwaves, the:** radio broadcasting time, from the literal meaning of *airwaves,* the waves of energy that are used for broadcasting radio programs. Page 95.

**Alaskan Radio Experimental Expedition:** a 1,500-mile (2,400-kilometer) voyage conducted to provide data for correct mapping of the coastline between the northwestern shores of the continental US and the southern part of Alaska. The expedition resulted in photographs and navigational information to correct the previously mischarted coastline. Page 95.

**albeit:** although; even if. Page 34.

**alee:** on or towards the *lee* side, the side sheltered from the wind or away from the wind. Page 23.

**aloft:** up the mast or into the rigging of a sailing vessel. *Call (someone) aloft* means have a person go aloft, as in order to move sails or otherwise handle the rigging. Page 23.

**American Fiction Guild:** a national organization of magazine fiction writers and novelists in the United States in the 1930s. L. Ron Hubbard was the president of the New York chapter in 1936. (A *guild* is an organization of persons with related interests, goals, etc., especially one formed for mutual aid or protection.) Page 34.

**Antony:** Mark Antony (83?–30 B.C.), Roman general and politician. After the assassination of Caesar (44 B.C.), Antony addresses the Roman people in a famous speech, as presented in the play *Julius Caesar* (1599) by English author William Shakespeare. By presenting Caesar as generous and loving, Antony persuades the people that his death was wrong and causes them to turn against Caesar's murderers. Page 154.

**apings:** instances of copying somebody or something in an absurd or mindless way. Page 129.

**aplomb:** showing self-confidence or assurance in oneself. Page 109.

**appropriated:** took for one's own use; took possession of. Page 8.

**Arabian Nights, The:** or *A Thousand and One Nights,* a collection of stories from Persia, Arabia, India and Egypt, compiled over hundreds of years. They include the stories of Aladdin and Ali Baba and have become particularly popular in Western countries. Page 78.

**arbor:** a crisscross framework or other structure used to support plants such as grapevines. Page 104.

**Argosy:** an American fiction magazine published by the Frank A. Munsey Company, first produced in the late 1800s. Containing science fiction, fantasy and other genres, *Argosy* featured some of the best adventure writers of the twentieth century. (The word *argosy* originally meant a large merchant ship and figuratively came to mean a rich, plentiful store or supply of something.) Page 62.

**assembly:** a signal, such as with a bugle or drum, for soldiers or other personnel to gather. Page 20.

**astro:** of or pertaining to the stars; taking place outside the Earth's atmosphere. Page 137.

**asunder:** into parts or pieces. Page 122.

**aught:** anything at all; anything whatever. Page 23.

**automatic:** a type of pistol having a mechanism that throws out the empty shell, puts in a new one and prepares the pistol to be fired again. A *service automatic* is an automatic issued by one of the armed services. Page 84.

**Avalon:** a resort town on Santa Catalina Island (an island off the coast of Southern California). Page 125.

**backwoods:** a sparsely inhabited, forested area distant from the main centers of population. Page 108.

**ballad(s):** a story in poetic form, often of folk origin and intended to be sung. Page 8.

**bane:** something that causes death, destruction or ruin. Page 101.

**bard:** a poet, especially a person who composed and recited epic or heroic poems, often while playing the harp or the like. Page 199.

**baritone:** a deep-sounding male voice. Page 95.

**barnacled:** covered with *barnacles*, small marine organisms with a shell that cling to rocks and ships and draw food by extending slender hairs through their shell to catch small organisms. Page 101.

**Bataan:** a peninsula on the west part of Luzon, the chief island of the Philippines. Page 113.

**bauble:** something that is small and decorative but of little real value. Page 122.

**beam:** the full width of a ship at its widest point. Page 99.

**beckoned:** extended interest or attraction to (someone or something); tempted. Page 33.

**becks:** calls or summons with a gesture. Page 151.

**bees, yellow:** an allusion to the yellow-painted taxis found in great number in New York City. Page 37.

**beetles, green:** an allusion to the trolley buses (electric buses powered from overhead wires) that were a common form of public transport in New York City from the late 1800s until the 1940s. Such trolley buses were often painted green and cost a dime (10 cents) to ride. Page 37.

**beguiled:** misled or deluded. Page 160.

**beleaguered:** surrounded with an army so as to prevent escape; hemmed in. Page 113.

**bellied:** figuratively, swelled or filled as from carrying something. Page 83.

***Beowulf:*** an epic poem thought to have been written in the eighth century by an unknown author, considered the greatest poem of that era. The poem is more than 3,000 lines long and is written in Old English. Page 35.

**bequeath:** to pass (something) on to another; hand down. Page 153.

**bier:** a frame or stand on which a corpse or the coffin containing it is laid before burial. Page 152.

**bilged, fumy-:** having its *bilge,* the area inside the bottom of a boat, full of *fumes,* gas having a strong, unpleasant odor and that is dangerous to breathe, here used in reference to gasoline fumes (which are explosive) filling the bilge. Page 98.

**black cat:** a reference to the belief that a black cat brings bad luck, especially if it passes in front of a person. In earlier times, black cats were regarded as evil spirits and were associated with witches. Page 78.

**Blackfeet:** a group of Native North American peoples including the Blackfeet of Montana and several tribes now living in Canada. This group controlled areas that were fought over by fur traders in the 1800s. Page 8.

**blare:** 1. loud sound; also, make a loud sound. Page 38.
2. dazzling color and brilliance. Page 79.

**blast:** 1. an explosion caused by the shooting of a weapon. Page 20.
2. strongly blowing wind. Page 101.

**blaze:** a trail or road marked out by spots or signs made on trees, as by painting, making a cut in or by chipping away a piece of the bark. Used figuratively. Page 63.

**blood brother:** either one of two men or boys who have sworn mutual loyalty and friendship, typically by a ritual or ceremony involving a superficial cut in the skin and the mingling (mixing) of each other's blood. Page 8.

**blues:** a form of music expressing despair, mainly slow, sad songs, developed from African-American folk songs in the early twentieth century. Page 167.

**Boeing:** a United States aircraft company founded in 1916 that became one of the world's largest manufacturers of military and commercial aircraft. Named after its founder, William E. Boeing (1881–1956). Page 82.

**bolster (one's) sway:** support and make stronger someone's rule or control over a person, group or area. Page 109.

**bosun:** an officer on a ship whose job is to supervise maintenance of the ship and its equipment. Page 103.

**brace, spring sure after:** of the rigging (ropes, chains, etc.) on a sailing vessel, to move suddenly (spring) into a stable (sure) position after a *brace,* an action or instance of moving the sail or sails on a ship so as to change the ship's direction by use of ropes, also known as *braces.* On a large ship, bracing is a highly intricate maneuver requiring the majority of the ship's crew due to the immense force involved when the wind is blowing against the sails. Page 23.

**braves:** Native North American warriors. Page 19.

**brawling:** making a deep, loud, roaring sound, as the wind or water. Page 101.

**bray:** a loud, harsh-sounding voice. Page 109.

**brayed:** made a loud, harsh sound, like a donkey. Page 20.

**breasted:** opposed or fought against boldly; dealt with in a determined way. Page 126.

**Bremerton:** a city in western Washington, a state in the northwest United States, on the Pacific coast. The large US Naval Yard in Bremerton was established in 1891 and provides maintenance for every class of naval vessel. Page 9.

**brigade(s):** in the Canadian and US fur trade, a convoy of canoes, sleds, wagons or pack animals used to supply trappers during the eighteenth and nineteenth centuries. Page 8.

**brink:** a crucial or critical point, especially of a situation or state beyond which catastrophe occurs. Page 143.

**Brisbane:** a city and seaport in the eastern part of Australia. The city lies along the Brisbane River, near the Pacific Ocean, and is a major port and manufacturing center. Page 113.

**Browning, Robert:** (1812–1889) English poet, noted for his finely drawn character studies in a style of poetry he developed called *dramatic monologues.* In these poems, Browning speaks in the voice of an imaginary or historical character at a dramatic moment in that person's life. Page 8.

**bucko:** young man; fellow. Page 17.

***Buckskin Brigades:*** a novel by L. Ron Hubbard, published (1937) by The Macaulay Publishing Company and hailed as a first-ever authentic description of Native North American people and their way of life. Set in the early 1800s, the story centers on the Blackfeet Indians, a powerful Native American nation threatened by the fur trade and by white men intent on trapping beaver for the fur, a valuable commodity in Europe. The trappers build forts and organize brigades (convoys of canoes, sleds, wagons or pack animals used to supply trappers), all without regard for either the Indians or the environment. Page 8.

**bucolic:** 1. of or characteristic of the natural beauty found in the country or the pleasant, simple ways of country life. Page ix.
2. having a rough and unrefined appearance, as is characteristic of farming regions. Page 109.

**bugle:** a military instrument of brass or copper, resembling the trumpet, but smaller and used in the army to call soldiers. Page 20.

**bull(s):** a formal command issued by one in authority. Page 109.

**bunion(s):** a painful swelling of the big toe, often caused by walking with poorly fitted shoes, that can be painful to someone traveling on foot. Page 82.

**Burroughs, Edgar Rice:** (1875–1950) American writer best known for creating the character Tarzan in his novel *Tarzan of the Apes,* which appeared in 1914. Burroughs also wrote science fiction novels. Along with his twenty-six Tarzan stories, he wrote a total of more than seventy books. Page 33.

**burthen:** an older form of *burden,* here meaning the carrying capacity of a ship. Page 99.

**butte:** a hill or mountain standing alone and rising abruptly above the surrounding land. Page 17.

**by the same token:** in like manner; similarly. Page 58.

*C*

**cab:** 1. an informal term for a *taxicab,* a car whose driver is paid to transport passengers, typically for short distances. Page 45.
2. the covered compartment of a heavy vehicle or machine, such as a truck or locomotive, in which the operator or driver sits. Page 49.

**cabbie:** an informal term for a taxicab driver. Page 45.

**Cable Censor Office:** during World War II (1939–1945), a part of the US Navy that censored cable communications in order to prevent the relay of sensitive data to the enemy. A *cable* is a type of telegram sent by underwater wires. Page 113.

**cadence:** a rhythmic sequence or flow of sounds in language, especially a particular rhythmic sequence distinctive of a type, style or time period of poetry or other forms of writing. Page 35.

**Caesar:** Gaius Julius Caesar (100?–44 B.C.), Roman general and statesman. His conquests helped establish the huge empire ruled by Rome and his political ambitions led to his being appointed Roman dictator for life. He was assassinated in 44 B.C. by political enemies who feared he would try to make himself a king, thereby destroying the existing Roman government. Page 154.

**Campbell, Jr., John W.:** (1910–1971) American editor and writer who began writing science fiction while at college. In 1937 Campbell was appointed editor of the magazine *Astounding Stories,* later titled *Astounding Science Fiction* and then *Analog.* Under his editorship *Astounding* became a major influence in the development of science fiction and published stories by some of the most important writers of that time. Page 62.

**camp, made:** put up a tent or arranged other temporary means of shelter when sleeping outdoors. Page 24.

**cannery fleet:** a group of fishing vessels that supply fish to a *cannery,* a factory for putting fish into cans. Canneries have existed in ports such as Ketchikan since the late 1800s, mainly handling the salmon that are fished in the area. Page 98.

**canted:** spoke in insincere terms. Page 119.

**canvas:** the extent, scope or background of something, as a life, a series of events, etc. Likened to a piece of *canvas,* a strong, heavy, closely woven fabric on which a painting is done. Page 8.

**Caribbean Motion Picture Expedition:** a voyage organized in the early 1930s by L. Ron Hubbard aboard the sailing vessel *Doris Hamlin.* With the roughly fifty students who sailed with him, LRH toured and captured on film a number of picturesque Caribbean ports. Page 9.

**carrion:** dead or decaying flesh. Page 13.

**caskets, black:** an allusion to *limousines,* large, usually black, luxurious automobiles, often chauffeur driven. A *casket* is a rectangular box or chest for a corpse to be buried in, especially one that is ornamented and lined. Page 37.

**castaway:** a person who has been shipwrecked or set adrift. Page 28.

**catalytic:** also *catalyst,* a substance that increases the rate of a chemical reaction without itself undergoing any change. Page 130.

**cayuse:** a horse, especially an Indian pony. Page 17.

**Chacon, Cape:** the southeastern point of Prince of Wales Island, Alaska. Ketchikan is further north, on an adjacent island. Page 108.

**Chandler, Raymond:** (1888–1959) American author of crime and detective stories, mostly set in Los Angeles during the 1930s and 1940s. Page 33.

**cheek, turn the other:** accept injuries or insult without seeking revenge; refuse to retaliate. Page 163.

**Chilkat Bay:** a body of water in southeastern Alaska. Page 104.

**chine(s):** the line of intersection between the side and the bottom of a flat or V-bottom hull on a boat. Page 125.

**chivalric:** of or related to *chivalry,* the noble qualities and customs a knight was supposed to have, such as courage, honor and a readiness to help the weak and protect women. Page 123.

**circuits:** divisions of one's own mind which seem to make up other personalities and these other personalities affect one and argue with one and so forth. Page 145.

**clay, turned to:** used figuratively, had a hidden or unexpected weakness or frailty. Page 21.

**clerkly:** of or pertaining to one who is a clerk (an older term for a scholar). Page 61.

**click with:** function or fit well together with (something else); succeed or be successful with. Page 33.

**collective:** of or characteristic of a group of individuals taken together. Page 182.

**combers:** long, high waves that roll over or crash onto a beach. Page 125.

**commensurate:** corresponding in measure, size or amount. Page 8.

**commingle:** mix things together so that they become physically united or form a new combination. Page 185.

**conceit:** an exaggerated opinion of oneself, one's merits, etc.; vanity. Page 11.

**constraining:** limiting or restricting, as by the prevention of free expression. Page 62.

**contrary:** actively opposed to one's well-being or interests; antagonistic, hostile. Page 78.

**contrived:** obviously planned or calculated. Page 7.

**Conway, Peggy:** (?–1957) actress and entertainer who starred in the stage play of *Peg O' My Heart,* a play written in the early 1900s by English playwright John Hartley Manner (1870–1928). She performed for the USO (United Service Organizations) during World War II (1939–1945) and visited combat areas wearing a jacket bearing almost every regimental insignia. During the 1950s she worked in South Africa with South African officials as a personal representative of LRH. Page 150.

**corporal:** of or relating to the human body. Page 135.

**counterpoint, at:** as a contrasting but parallel element, item or theme. Page 113.

**court:** 1. attempt to win the support or favor of. Also, risk incurring (misfortune) because of the way one behaves. Page 179.
2. show that one is interested in something or wants to become involved in something. Page 186.

**coyote(s):** a wild animal of the dog family, native to North America, distinguished from the wolf by its relatively small size and slender build, large ears and narrow muzzle. Page 17.

**cramming:** a characteristic in which many things are crushed, crowded or tightly packed together. Page 12.

**cum:** combined with. Page 95.

**cupidity:** excessive desire to possess something; greed. Page 13.

**curlew:** any of several large brownish shorebirds with long legs and a long, downcurved bill. Page 23.

**curvetted:** leaped and frisked about. Page 137.

**Custer:** George Armstrong Custer (1839–1876), American soldier and general. He and his troops were killed in a battle with Sioux and Cheyenne warriors at the Little Bighorn River in southern Montana. Page 8.

**Davy:** Davy Jones, the spirit of the sea in sailors' legends and an allusion to the grave of those who perish at sea. Page 104.

**demimondaine:** pertaining to a class of women who have lost their standing in respectable society due to indiscreet behavior or sexual promiscuity. Page 109.

**demise:** the end of existence or activity. Page 8.

**demonity:** something regarded as a *demon*, a spirit; a devil. Page 135.

**Dent, Lester:** (1904–1959) American pulp fiction writer best known as the author of a series of stories on Doc Savage, a superhuman scientist and adventurer. Page 33.

**depth charge:** a large can filled with explosive material designed to sink and explode at a certain depth, used to destroy submarines. Page 113.

**diagrammatic:** in the form of an explanatory drawing or chart. Page 7.

**Dianetics:** Dianetics is a forerunner and substudy of Scientology. Dianetics means "through the mind" or "through the soul" (from Greek *dia,* through and *nous,* mind or soul). It is a system of coordinated axioms which resolve problems concerning human behavior and psychosomatic illnesses. It combines a workable technique and a thoroughly validated method for increasing sanity, by erasing unwanted sensations and unpleasant emotions. Page 1.

**divergent:** showing or having differences. Page 2.

**divination:** the methods or practice of attempting to foretell the future or discover the unknown through omens or supernatural powers. Page 78.

**do-and-dare:** reflecting or characterized by a determination to accomplish something and to be brave enough to do whatever is needed in order to accomplish it. Page 7.

**dog, midnight:** the midnight watch or shift. Page 23.

**dome(s):** a slang term for the head. Page 141.

**doom:** dreadful fate, especially death or utter ruin. Page 81.

**Dover shore:** an area on Vancouver Island, British Columbia, roughly 500 miles (800 kilometers) south of Ketchikan, Alaska. Page 99.

**dowered:** provided with a *dower,* or *dowry,* the money, goods or property that a wife brings to her husband at marriage. Page 61.

**drear:** an older word used in poetry meaning dreary, melancholy. Page 119.

**drivel:** silly or meaningless talk or thinking; nonsense. Page 129.

**drum, tossing:** a reference to a buoy that is *tossing,* being moved repeatedly up and down or side to side by the waves. A *buoy* is an anchored float serving as a navigation mark, to show hazards or for mooring. Buoys mark channels (passageways for boats or ships), safe waterways and dangerous areas such as rocks, shallow waters and wrecks. They come in different shapes, sizes and colors, have various colored and timed flashing lights and sometimes have numbers and letters on them. Buoys are marked on a navigation chart with their colors, shapes and identifying letters or numbers and flashing light patterns. Page 104.

**dubbed:** had a descriptive name given to something. Page 95.

**Dundas Bay:** a bay in southeastern Alaska, located in Glacier Bay National Park, northwest of Juneau. Page 99.

**Earth Day International:** a worldwide observance held on April 22 each year. It began in 1970 to increase public awareness of environmental problems. Page 180.

**ebbing:** moving away from the land; receding. Page 100.

**eddy:** water moving in a direction that is against the flow of the tide; a contrary current. Page 103.

**elegy:** a mournful or reflective poem. Page 128.

**embittered:** characterized by strong feelings of hatred, resentment, intense antagonism or hostility. Page 8.

**Encinitas:** a coastal town in Southern California, established in the late 1800s. Page 33.

**engram:** a mental image picture which is a recording of a moment of pain and unconsciousness. This recording can be later brought into play by a similar word or environment and causes the individual to act as though in the presence of danger. They force the individual into patterns of thinking and behavior which are not called for by a reasonable appraisal of the situation. Page 142.

**entheta:** a compound word meaning *enturbulated theta,* theta in a turbulent state, agitated or disturbed. (*Theta* is the energy of thought and life. Theta is reason, serenity, stability, happiness, cheerful emotion, persistence and the other factors which Man ordinarily considers desirable.) Page 141.

**envelope, pushing the:** stretching the limits; accomplishing more than is considered possible. Page 35.

**epic:** characteristic of a long poem written in a grand style, especially one that expresses the ideals, important traditions and events relating to a person, group or the like. Page 168.

**e're:** also *ere,* before or earlier in time than (an older word, used in poetry). Page 21.

**erstwhile:** former; of times past. Page 144.

**eschew:** keep away from; avoid; shun. Page 140.

**etched:** engraved, usually on or as if on metal. *Etching* is a procedure used to reproduce images with a technique whereby part of the metal surface is "eaten away" by acid, leaving an impression of the image that can then be reproduced. Page 34.

**ethnological:** of or having to do with the science that analyzes cultures, especially in regard to their historical development and the similarities and dissimilarities between them. Page 8.

**ethnologist:** a person who specializes in *ethnology,* the science that analyzes cultures, especially in regard to their historical development and the similarities and dissimilarities between them. Page 78.

**eulogy:** a formal piece of writing in honor of a person who has recently died. Page 150.

**existential:** involving or concerned with human existence, as for example by describing circumstances, problems, questions or the like that relate to human existence. Page 8.

**Explorers Club:** an organization, headquartered in New York and founded in 1904, devoted exclusively to promoting the science of exploration. To further this aim, it provides grants for those who wish to participate in field research projects and expeditions. It has provided logistical support for some of the twentieth century's most daring expeditions. L. Ron Hubbard was a lifetime member of the Explorers Club. Page 95.

**Explorers Club flag:** a flag awarded to active members of the Explorers Club who are in command of, or serving with, expeditions that further the cause of exploration and field science. Since 1918 the Explorers Club flag has been carried on hundreds of expeditions, including those to both North and South Poles, the summit of Mount Everest and the surface of the Moon. Many famous persons in history have carried the Explorers Club flag, including L. Ron Hubbard. Page 95.

**exterior:** situated outside of the body. Page 135.

**extricate:** free or release from a confining, difficult or undesirable condition or situation. Page 161.

**factory hands:** people engaged in manual labor in a *factory,* a building or buildings where goods are manufactured or assembled chiefly by machine. Page 58.

**Fairlight:** a computer-based musical instrument consisting of a processor, a memory bank and a keyboard. It digitally records any sound from a microphone, tape machine or other sound source, and then reproduces it by way of its musical keyboard. Any sound so recorded into the Fairlight will then conform to the notes of the keyboard and can be played as musical notes. The creator of the instrument named it after a ferryboat in Sydney, Australia, called the *Fairlight*. Page 167.

**fandango:** a lively Spanish or Spanish-American dance. Page 137.

**far-flung:** extended far or to a great distance; remote. Page 1.

**fathom(s):** a unit of length equal to 6 feet (1.8 meters), used chiefly in nautical measurements. Page 99.

**fattened on:** became fat, as by feeding on. Page 155.

**Feds:** federal officials or law enforcement officers. Page 108.

**fisherfolk:** people who catch fish for a living. Page 96.

**fission:** the splitting of the central part of an atom (nucleus) into fragments. The pieces of the nucleus then strike other nuclei (centers of atoms) and cause them to fission (split), thus creating a chain reaction, which is accompanied by a significant release of energy. Page 182.

***Five-Novels Monthly:*** a pulp magazine published from 1928 until the late 1940s. The monthly schedule was continued until 1943, when paper shortages during World War II (1939–1945) forced it to a quarterly schedule and a resultant name change to *Five Novels* magazine. Page 82.

**foil:** a long, thin sword with a light, flexible blade, used in fencing matches. Used figuratively to refer to the quality of being extremely sharp, sensitive, perceptive or the like, as in seeing, thinking, understanding, etc. Page 168.

**formula(s):** any fixed or conventional method for doing something. Page 33.

**free verse:** poetry that does not rhyme or have a regular rhythm. Page 3.

**fumy-bilged:** having its *bilge,* the area inside the bottom of a boat, full of *fumes,* gas having a strong, unpleasant odor and that is dangerous to breathe, here used in reference to gasoline fumes (which are explosive) filling the bilge. Page 98.

**'gainst:** an older, shortened form of *against,* opposite in the course or direction of. Page 152.

**gallant:** brave; heroic. Page 100.

**George Washington University:** a private university, founded in 1821, in the city of Washington, DC. Named after the first president of the United States, George Washington (1732–1799), it maintains various schools of education, including the School of Engineering and Applied Science and the Columbian College of Arts and Sciences. The university has a long history of supporting research in physics and other technical fields. Page 7.

**Gettysburg Address:** a famous speech delivered in 1863 by United States President Abraham Lincoln (1809–1865). The occasion was the dedication of a soldiers' cemetery in Gettysburg, a south-central Pennsylvania town which, in July 1863, was the site of a major battle in the American Civil War (1861–1865). The speech aligned the purposes of the nation, presenting the heroism of the fallen soldiers with the need to uphold the principle they had fought for, "that government of the people, by the people, for the people, shall not perish from the earth." Page 154.

**giddy:** foolishly light; governed by wild or thoughtless impulses. Page 91.

**glen:** a narrow valley. Used figuratively. Page 119.

**goat:** a person who is blamed for the wrongdoings or mistakes of others; scapegoat. Page 106.

**God, to:** a shortening of the phrase "I wish to God," used in expressing a strong desire or hope. Page 29.

**gorge:** a narrow steep-walled canyon. Page 14.

**grade:** a step or degree in the state or condition of something, likened to a gradient or slope on a railroad or road. Page 152.

**grade, make the pulp:** succeed by reaching the goal of having one's writing published in pulp magazines. Page 58.

**Great Depression:** a drastic decline in the world economy starting in the United States, resulting in mass unemployment and widespread poverty that lasted from 1929 until 1939. Page 33.

**Great Flood:** the story of a massive flood that covered the Earth thousands of years ago. The flood destroyed all living things except those that God permitted to survive. Similar stories are found in the religious traditions of many peoples, including Native Americans, peoples of the Middle East and southern Asia and others. Page 95.

**green beetles:** an allusion to the trolley buses (electric buses powered from overhead wires) that were a common form of public transport in New York City from the late 1800s until the 1940s. Such trolley buses were often painted green and cost a dime (10 cents) to ride. Page 37.

**grist for (one's) mill:** something that is to one's advantage or profit. *Grist* is grain that is to be ground up. Page 48.

**guidon:** a small flag, broad at one end and pointed or forked at the other end, originally carried by the military for identification. Page 123.

**gull:** seabirds having long wings, slender legs, webbed feet, a strong, hooked bill and feathers of chiefly white and gray. Also called *sea gull.* Page 101.

**gunboat:** a small ship that carries guns fixed on the deck, for use in shallow coastal waters and rivers. Page 14.

**gutted:** that has had the contents (resources, goods, etc.) removed, as by force. Page 128.

**guttered:** literally of a fire or flame, flickered when on the point of being extinguished. Used figuratively of something becoming gradually weaker, less viable or the like. Page 120.

**gyrates:** motions in a circle or spiral. Page 137.

**hacked:** cut with heavy blows in an irregular or random fashion. Used figuratively. Page 63.

**haiku:** a form of Japanese verse which has seventeen syllables divided into three lines of five, seven and five syllables, often presenting aspects of nature and containing a reference to a season of the year. These poems merely suggest ideas and feelings so that the reader must use imagination to interpret them. Page 8.

**Hammett, Dashiell:** (1894–1961) highly influential American author of detective novels. Drawing on his years of work as a private detective, Hammett began writing in the early 1920s. With his realistic writing style, he created enduringly popular characters and plots, with a number of his best-known works, such as *The Maltese Falcon* (1930), later adapted for film. Page 33.

**hands, factory:** people engaged in manual labor in a *factory,* a building or buildings where goods are manufactured or assembled chiefly by machine. Page 58.

**hard-boiled:** down-to-earth, practical, realistic; tough; not affected by sentiment, pity, etc. Page 33.

**hard by:** close by; very near. Page 126.

**hard under:** going beneath the waves (under) to an extreme degree. Page 23.

**hast:** an old form of saying *have;* used with *thou* (you) to mean you have. Page 151.

**H-bomb:** *hydrogen bomb,* an explosive weapon of mass destruction (far more powerful than an atomic bomb), that derives its energy from the fusion (combining) of hydrogen atoms. H-bombs were first developed and exploded by the United States and Russia in the early 1950s. Page 156.

**heady:** having a strong or exhilarating effect. Page 91.

**heart of oak:** a courageous spirit, said of a person capable of resistance or endurance. Said in reference to the wood of the oak tree because of its hardness and enduring quality. Page 101.

**Hecate Straits:** a wide but shallow channel immediately south of Alaska and lying just off the coast of Canada. Page 99.

**Helena:** city and capital of Montana, a state in the northwestern United States bordering on Canada. Page 7.

**helmsman:** the person in charge of steering a ship. The helmsman is stationed at the *helm,* the wheel by which the ship is steered. Also called *steersman.* Page 14.

**herein:** in this writing, document or the like. Page 1.

**hi:** an exclamation used to call attention. Page 17.

**high-sea:** of or having to do with the *high seas,* the open, unenclosed waters of any sea or ocean, especially such waters that are not within any country's jurisdiction. Page 2.

**hitherto:** up to this time; until now. Page 135.

**homing:** a going or returning to one's home. Page 101.

**Homo sapiens:** Mankind; human beings. Page 154.

**hopscotch, played:** moved as if by jumping from one position to another, as in playing *hopscotch,* a children's game using a pattern of squares marked on the ground. Each child throws a stone into a square, then jumps on one leg and jumps along the empty squares to pick up the stone again. Page 45.

**horny:** toughened and calloused, as hands that have areas of hard thickened skin. Page 23.

**horseshoe(s):** a flat U-shaped piece of iron, regarded as a symbol of good luck. Literally, horseshoes are nailed to the bottom of a horse's hooves to protect them against hard surfaces. Page 78.

**hulk:** a heavy ship that is difficult to steer. Page 107.

**hysteria:** a state of extreme or exaggerated emotion such as excitement or panic, especially among large numbers of people. Page 130.

**idol:** an image such as one made of wood or stone used as an object of worship. Page 106.

**imagery:** figurative description or illustration, used in literature to call up images in the mind. Page 34.

**imagist:** of *imagism,* a movement in poetry in England and the United States during the early 1900s that was initiated by American poet Ezra Pound. The movement sought to modernize poetry by using ordinary language, having complete freedom in subject matter and presenting clear, precise and sharp images. Page 35.

**immaterial:** that does not matter; not pertinent; unimportant. Page 1.

**incisive:** sharp, keen, penetrating. Page 8.

**India ink:** a type of liquid black ink that is made from a coloring agent and formed into cakes or sticks. To use the ink, the cake or stick is moistened with water. The resulting ink is applied with a brush, both for drawing and for writing the letters of the Japanese language. Page 113.

**inland waterway:** a natural protected channel (also called *Inside Passage*) in northwestern North America, 950 miles (1,500 kilometers) long. This waterway extends along the coast from Seattle, Washington, past British Columbia, Canada, to the southern area of Alaska. The passage is made up of a series of channels running between the mainland and a string of islands on the west that protect the passage from Pacific Ocean storms. Page 95.

**in scan:** within view. Page 100.

**insouciantly:** in a cheerfully unconcerned, carefree way. Page 138.

**instrument:** something or somebody used as a means of achieving a desired result or accomplishing a particular purpose. Page 130.

**interned:** confined as a prisoner. Page 162.

**intrinsic:** belonging to something as one of the basic and essential elements that make it what it is. Page 168.

**invoking:** putting (something) into use. Page 154.

**irascible:** easily angered; quick-tempered. Page 62.

**irradiate:** expose or overexpose to radiation. Page 182.

**Java:** the main island of Indonesia, northwest of Australia. Page 113.

*jibaro:* a person from a rural area of Puerto Rico. Page 84.

**jingles:** words or verses arranged so as to have obvious, easy rhythm and simple repetitions, as in some poetry. Page 138.

**joust:** literally, combat between two knights on horseback with lances (long, pointed weapons). Also used to mean an action resembling that, especially in a personal struggle or competition. Page 122.

**Juneau:** port and capital city of the state of Alaska, located in the southeastern part of the state. Page 96.

**keel:** the long piece of wood or steel along the bottom of a boat that forms the major part of its structure and helps to keep the boat balanced in the water. Page 23.

**ketch:** a two-masted sailing boat with sails set lengthwise (fore and aft) and with the mast closer to the front taller than the mast behind. Page 95.

**Ketchikan:** a seaport in southeastern Alaska, one of the chief ports on Alaska's Pacific coast. Ketchikan is a transportation and communications center. Page 95.

**KGBU:** the group of letters (termed *call letters*) that identify a radio transmitting station, in this case the public radio station located in Ketchikan, Alaska. Radio KGBU operated from the late 1920s until the early 1940s. It was the second radio station in Alaska. Page 95.

**kindred:** of like nature; similar. Page 159.

**knoll:** a small rounded hill. Page 19.

**Koenig photometer:** an early device that gave a visual representation of sound waves, invented by German physicist Karl Rudolf Koenig (1832–1901). It allowed one to make a record of and compare the wavelengths of different spoken sounds. Page 7.

**Kowtung Gorge:** also spelled *Qutang,* a five-mile-long gorge (a narrow steep-walled canyon), the most magnificent and dangerous of the famous Three Gorges, located in the upper (western) section of the Yangtze River. Page 14.

**Krishna:** an important Hindu god who appeared as an incarnation (living being embodying a deity or spirit) of Vishnu, one of the three main gods of the Hindu religion. Page 162.

**lair:** a bed or resting place. Page 17.

**lament(s):** a formal expression of sorrow or mourning, especially in verse or in song. Page 154.

**lance(s):** a long wooden shaft with a pointed metal head, used as a weapon by knights and cavalry soldiers (soldiers on horseback) in charging. Page 17.

**lancet:** a small surgical knife. Page 13.

**larder:** a room or large cupboard for storing food. Page 142.

**lathered:** covered in white foam produced during periods of heavy sweating. Page 21.

**latitude(s):** a region of the earth considered in relation to its distance from the equator. Page 84.

**latterly:** at a subsequent time; later. Page 1.

**leading light:** someone who influences or sets an example to others. Page 2.

**league:** an older measurement of distance of variable length, usually about 3 miles (5 kilometers). Page 79.

**leering:** regarding someone in a sly, malicious or unpleasant manner. Used figuratively. Page 29.

**L'Envoi:** the final section of a book or play, or a short section at the end of a poem, used for summing up or as a dedication. *L'* is French for the, and *envoi* means a sending. Page 107.

**lieutenant (junior grade):** a commissioned officer in the US Navy who is directly above an ensign, the lowest commissioned officer, and directly below a lieutenant. (A *commission* is a document conferring authority to officers in the army, navy and other military services, issued by the president of the United States.) Page 113.

**line, parting:** a rope (line) that is breaking, so that, for example, a ship is no longer tied or secured. Page 125.

**Lion's Gate:** a bridge connecting two sections of Vancouver, a city in southwestern British Columbia. Page 104.

**list:** an enclosed arena for a contest between two mounted knights, charging with blunted lances in an attempt to knock each other off their horses. Used figuratively. Page 122.

**listless:** having or showing little or no interest in anything; not caring, apathetic. Page 45.

**Little Bighorn:** a river about 90 miles (145 kilometers) long, rising in the Bighorn Mountains of northern Wyoming and flowing north to the Bighorn River in southern Montana. Sioux and Cheyenne warriors defeated the forces of General George A. Custer in the Little Bighorn valley on June 25, 1876. Page 8.

**lobbied:** attempted to persuade influential persons to support something. Page 34.

**long-biding:** continuing or lasting for a long time. Page 168.

**loomed large:** was regarded as significant, from the literal meaning of *loomed,* appeared, took shape or came in sight, especially in a large or important way. Page 8.

**looms:** comes into view, shows up, as if in a magnified, almost threatening manner. Page 182.

**lore:** accumulated facts, traditions or beliefs about a particular subject. Page 9.

**lorgnette:** a pair of eyeglasses held in the hand, usually by a long metal or ivory handle. Page 57.

**lotus:** in Greek mythology, a fruit that induced blissful forgetfulness and dreamy contentment in those who ate it. Page 23.

**lunar:** of or pertaining to the moon; influenced by or dependent upon the moon. Page 137.

**Lutine bell:** the bell salvaged from the British warship *Lutine,* wrecked in 1799 with the loss of everyone aboard. The bell is located in the insurance office of Lloyd's of London and is traditionally rung prior to any announcement of a ship overdue or lost at sea. Page 99.

**lyrics:** the words of a song. Page 1.

**magnate:** literally, a person having wealth and influence; also, a business, enterprise or the like having influence or distinction. Page 33.

**magnum opus:** a large or important literary work. A Latin expression, the term literally means great work. Page 167.

**maiden:** a young unmarried woman. Page 23.

**mail buoy:** a *buoy* is an anchored float serving as a navigation mark, to show hazards or for mooring. A "mail buoy" is a prank used on naval ships in which new recruits are told to stand watch at the bow of the ship for a buoy that passing ships supposedly attach mail to. Used humorously as the name of LRH's radio program in Ketchikan, Alaska, a program in which listeners' questions were taken up and answered. Page 95.

**main:** the *mainmast,* the principal mast of a ship. Page 23.

**mainsul:** representing a nautical pronunciation of *mainsail,* the principal sail of a ship. Page 23.

**make the pulp grade:** succeed by reaching the goal of having one's writing published in pulp magazines. Page 58.

**mark:** any of the lines on the side of a vessel that form a scale of measurement. These marks enable one to tell how deep a ship sits in the water. A *"fathom mark and two"* would indicate that the ship sat in the water to a depth of a fathom mark (6 feet or 1.8 meters) plus 2 feet (.6 meter), for a total of 8 feet (2.4 meters). Page 99.

**marquee:** a large tent, often square or rectangular, having a high, slanted roof and with sides that could be rolled up or let down. Page 123.

**McIntyre, O. O.:** Oscar Odd McIntyre (1884–1938), New York City newspaper columnist and critic. Page 58.

**mecca:** a place regarded as supremely sacred or valuable. Also, a place that is regarded as fashionable and which is an important center for a particular activity or one that is visited by a great many people. Page 33.

**Medford Lakes:** a town in south central New Jersey, a state in the eastern United States, on the Atlantic Ocean. Page 135.

**medieval:** characteristic of or in the style of the *Middle Ages,* a period in the history of Europe that lasted from about the late 400s to the mid-1400s. Stories and poems about historic figures such as Alexander the Great (356–323 B.C.) and about knights and their brave deeds achieved great popularity, especially during the late medieval period. Page 35.

**Messiah:** one who is expected to deliver the world from suffering and bring an era of peace and justice. Page 162.

**MEST:** a word made up of the first letters of Matter, Energy, Space and Time. A coined word for the physical universe. Page 140.

**mimeographed:** produced through the use of a mimeograph, a machine that makes copies of written, drawn or typed material from a stencil. A *stencil* is a piece of plastic, metal or paper in which letters have been cut out and then inked so that their impressions are left on the surface of paper applied against the stencil. Page 138.

**minaret:** a tall, usually slender tower attached to a Muslim house of worship. Page 79.

**Miniver Cheevy:** a character described in a 1907 poem by American poet Edwin Arlington Robinson (1869–1935). The poem tells of Miniver and his longing for the Middle Ages, his scorn of money (although he is "sore annoyed without it") and his general feeling of having been born out of his time. Page 123.

**Model T:** an automobile manufactured by the Ford Motor Company, the first motor vehicle successfully mass-produced on an assembly line. Model Ts were produced between 1908 and 1927. Page 24.

**Montana:** a state in the western United States, bordering with Canada on the north. The western part of the state is mountainous and the eastern portion is a gently rolling landscape with grazing cattle and sheep. L. Ron Hubbard lived in Montana as a young boy. Page 1.

**moor:** also *mooring,* something such as ropes, cables, an anchor or the like that secures a ship so that it does not float away from where it has been tied or anchored. Page 125.

**Moore, Catherine L.:** (1911–1987) an American writer of fantasy and science fiction novels and short stories. Her stories appeared in pulp magazines in the 1930s and in *Astounding Science Fiction* magazine throughout the 1940s. Moore was one of the first women to write in the genre, thus paving the way for many other female writers. Page 2.

**moral fiber:** strength of character, determination and courage; ethical principles. Page 189.

**mused:** said (something) in a thoughtful or questioning way. Page 131.

**musketry:** a military term for the technique or practice of using guns such as pistols and rifles, especially the practice of concentrating the collective fire of such guns against a target. Page 14.

**muted:** making little sound; quiet. Page 117.

**naught:** nothing at all. Page 29.

**naval yard:** also *navy yard,* a navy-owned *shipyard,* a place where warships are built and repaired. Page 9.

**'neath:** a chiefly literary form of the word *beneath.* Page 25.

**nigh:** nearly; almost. Page 126.

**Noah:** Biblical character instructed by God to build an ark (large rudderless ship) for his wife and family and a pair of each of Earth's animals. God, resolving to destroy the wickedness of people, then flooded Earth with forty days and forty nights of rain, drowning all living creatures. When the rain ceased and the water drained, Noah and the others began a new life on Earth. Page 95.

**nor'easter:** a storm with northeast winds. Page 125.

**nothing if not:** used to emphasize a particular quality that something has; above everything; undoubtedly. Page 2.

**notoriety:** a state of being widely and publicly known; famous. Page 96.

**oak, heart of:** a courageous spirit, said of a person capable of resistance or endurance. Said in reference to the wood of the oak tree because of its hardness and enduring quality. Page 101.

**Oak Knoll Naval Hospital:** a naval hospital located in Oakland, California, USA, where LRH spent time recovering from injuries sustained during World War II (1939–1945) and researching the effect of the mind on the physical recovery of patients. Page 123.

**Oakland:** a seaport in western California, on San Francisco Bay, opposite the city of San Francisco. Page 123.

**ode:** a poem, especially one that is written in praise of a particular person, thing or event. Page 145.

**o'er:** a contraction of the word *over. O'er* is a literary word, used for example in poetry. Page 19.

**ogle:** staring boldly and with obvious desire. Page 149.

**Ole Doc Methuselah:** science fiction stories by LRH about the adventures of the title character, a member of the elite Soldiers of Light organization dedicated to the preservation of Mankind, combating disease, corruption and the desperate perversities of human behavior along the intergalactic spaceways. Written under the pen name of Rene Lafayette, these stories appeared in *Astounding Science Fiction* between October 1947 and January 1950. Page 1.

**Olympic Mountains:** a mountain range in northwestern Washington State. The highest peak is Mount Olympus, which is 7,965 feet (2,428 meters) tall. The lower slopes of the range are heavily forested, while the peaks contain many small glaciers. Page 24.

**operatic:** of or pertaining to *opera,* a dramatic work presented on stage with music, the story being presented by actors who sing rather than speak their lines. Page 28.

**opiate allure:** an *opiate* is any of various illegal drugs derived from *opium,* a highly addictive drug extracted from the opium poppy. *Opiate allure* refers to the attractive or tempting quality (allure) of such drugs brought about by the false feeling of happiness or well-being they create and their highly addictive properties. Page 180.

**oration:** a formal speech made on a public occasion as part of a ceremony, such as for a funeral. Page 154.

**oratorical:** characterized by or using language to convey one's thoughts with clarity, grace and effectiveness. Page 154.

**oratorio:** a large-scale musical composition for voices and instruments that has a religious theme, often telling a sacred story, but without scenery, stage action or the like. Page 198.

**Pacific Northwest:** an area of the United States that includes the states of Washington, Oregon, Idaho and western Montana. Page 8.

**Pacific Theater:** the areas of the Pacific Ocean and the islands of the Pacific where fighting took place during World War II (1939–1945). Page 113.

**Page, Norvell:** (1904–1961) American pulp fiction writer, journalist and editor best known as the author of the majority of the adventures of the Spider, a crime fighter wanted by the law for executing his criminal antagonists. Page 33.

**paladin:** a knight or heroic champion; a legendary hero. Page 123.

**Panhandle:** part of the state of Alaska that extends along the Pacific coast, south from the main part of the state. A *panhandle* is a narrow section of land shaped like the handle of a cooking pan, that extends away from the body of the state it belongs to. Page 95.

**papier-mâché:** a material, made from paper pulp or shreds of paper mixed with glue or paste, that can be molded into various shapes when wet to form various objects such as figures, boxes, masks, etc. Page 122.

**parade, on:** on display, from *parade,* a review of troops. Page 20.

**paradox:** a situation that seems to have contradictory or inconsistent qualities. Page 135.

**parchment:** a stiff, strong paper that is smooth or textured and that is used for special documents, letters or artwork. Page 178.

**parting line:** a rope (line) that is breaking, so that, for example, a ship is no longer tied or secured. Page 125.

**PC-815:** a small, fast US Navy submarine chaser intended for antisubmarine warfare. (*PC* is an abbreviation of *Patrol Coastal.*) Page 113.

**pedestrian:** ordinary, unimaginative or uninspired. Page 33.

**pelf:** the things a person owns; property or belongings. Page 155.

**Peloponnesian dead:** in Pericles' famous eulogy, those Athenians who had died in 431 B.C., the first year of the *Peloponnesian War,* a conflict in ancient Greece between the rival cities of Athens and Sparta. Though Sparta was the ultimate winner, in 404 B.C., the early years of the war saw Athens the victor. (The name *Peloponnesian* refers to the *Peloponnesus,* the peninsula forming the southern part of the mainland of Greece, where Sparta was located.) Page 154.

**penguin:** a person wearing a dinner jacket; also, such a jacket. Page 67.

**pennon:** any flag or banner, such as the flags flown off the top of a ship's mast. Page 47.

**pensive:** thinking deeply about something, especially in a sad or serious way. Page 25.

**pent:** confined or restrained; not released. Page 49.

**perchance:** perhaps; possibly. Page 113.

**perennial:** lasting for a long time; enduring or continually recurring. Page 2.

**Pericles:** (495?–429 B.C.) Athenian statesman and general who led the city of Athens in its rise to power as a democratic state, bringing about a Golden Age of achievements in the arts and literature. In his famous eulogy of 431 B.C., he praised not only the brave who had died to protect Athens, but also the city itself, stating further that the living must strive to uphold the freedoms that their countrymen had died to preserve. *See also* **Peloponnesian dead.** Page 154.

**per se:** by or in itself, essentially; without reference to anything else. Page 1.

**personification:** the action of thinking of or representing a figure of an inanimate object as having life or personality or other human qualities. Also representing such as possessing human form. Page 108.

**perspective:** a visible scene, especially one extending to a distance; vista. Page 191.

**Phoenix, Arizona:** a city in and capital of Arizona, a state in the southwestern United States. During the early and mid-1950s, LRH gave approximately five hundred recorded lectures in Phoenix. Page 138.

**picketeer:** also *picketer,* a person stationed by a union or the like outside a factory, store, etc., in order to dissuade or prevent workers or customers from entering it during a strike. Page 70.

**pilot:** a person who is qualified to steer vessels through certain difficult waters. Page 14.

**pitted:** marked with or covered with holes, as from bombs. Page 154.

**placid:** pleasantly calm or peaceful; serene, quiet or undisturbed. Page 153.

**placidity:** the quality or state of being placid. *See also* **placid.** Page 61.

**plaintive:** expressing sorrow; sad-sounding. Page 167.

**plate windows:** windows made with *plate glass,* a strong, thick, clear glass in large sheets, used for store windows, mirrors, etc. Page 70.

**platform crowd:** the group of people waiting for a train at a *platform,* a raised structure along the side of a railway track where passengers get on and off trains. Page 49.

**platform, rolling:** a cart with a flat floor, supported on wheels, and with a rack mounted upon it. Clothing can be hung on the rack and thus moved from place to place. Page 65.

**plunder:** the action of taking things that belong to others by using violent and forceful methods. Page 155.

**Po Chü-i:** (772–846) a Chinese poet and government official. He was one of the greatest writers of the T'ang dynasty. Page 35.

**posthumously:** in a manner that is *posthumous,* occurring after the author's lifetime. Page 191.

**posturing:** the taking up of a policy, an attitude or an approach toward something, especially as intended to impress or mislead the public, other nations, etc. Page 154.

**Pound, Ezra:** (1885–1972) American poet, editor and translator, considered one of the foremost literary figures of the twentieth century. Page 35.

**preempted:** taken or used before someone else. Page 78.

**primeval:** of or relating to the earliest ages of the world or human history. Page 78.

**proliferation:** the action of making widely available, increasing in number or spreading something rapidly. Page 168.

**prose:** ordinary written language, in contrast to poetry. Page 35.

**protectorship:** the state of being protected or defended, used with reference to the status of Puerto Rico, an island in the Caribbean Sea associated with the United States and having self-government in local matters. Page 84.

**pudgy:** thick or fat. Page 70.

**Puerto Rico:** a self-governing island in the northern Caribbean Sea, associated with the United States since its acquisition from Spain in 1898. Puerto Rico is located 1,000 miles (1,600 kilometers) southeast of Florida. Page 84.

**Puget Sound:** a long, narrow bay of the Pacific Ocean on the coast of Washington, a state in the northwestern United States. Page 24.

**pugnacious:** combative; inclined to fight. Page 49.

**pulpateer:** a writer for the pulps, from the word *pulp* combined with the ending *-ateer,* a variation of *-eer,* a person who produces, handles or is otherwise significantly associated with (the pulps). Page 58.

**pulpwood stock:** the rough type of paper (stock) used for printing inexpensive magazines, etc. The low-cost pulp used in its manufacture is made from wood fibers, which give a rough texture. Page 33.

**punch the clock:** literally, put a time card in the time clock for noting time of arrival and departure. A *time clock* is a clock with an attachment that may be manually activated to punch or stamp the exact time on a card or tape, used to keep a record of the time of something, as of the arrival and departure of employees. Page 58.

**purple spread:** a *bedspread,* an attractive cover put on top of all the sheets and covers on a bed that is *purple,* traditionally the color reserved for the use of a ruler or other royal person. Page 61.

**quailed:** drew back in fear; lost courage. Page 81.

**quaint:** strange, peculiar or unusual in an interesting or amusing way. Page 78.

**quaver:** a trembling or shaking sound played from an instrument by alternating back and forth between two notes. Page 20.

**quay:** a platform that runs along the edge of a port or harbor, where boats are loaded and unloaded. Page 47.

**quest:** a search or pursuit made in order to find or obtain something. Page 182.

**quintessential:** representing the most perfect example. Page 108.

**race:** 1. move or progress swiftly. Page 23.

2. humanity considered as a whole, as in the human race. Page 115.

**racking:** showing great mental pain or stress. Page 11.

**rankers, top:** the most successful or respected people in a field or profession. Page 58.

**realized:** made real; given reality to. Page 78.

**red-light district:** an area or district in a city in which many houses of prostitution are located. Page 108.

**redoubtable:** that is to be honored or respected due to superior qualities. Page 129.

**rendering:** a work forming a presentation, expression or interpretation (as of an idea or theme). Page 78.

**replete:** abundantly supplied or provided; filled. Page 84.

**replicate:** do (something) again or copy (something); reproduce. Page 167.

**resplendently:** in a dazzlingly impressive manner; magnificently; splendidly. Page 149.

**rife:** in a full or abundant way; in large quantity. Page 23.

**Rigadoon:** a lively dance for one couple, characterized by a jumping step. Page 137.

**riggin':** an informal pronunciation of *rigging,* the system of ropes, chains, etc., used to support and control the masts and sails of a sailing vessel. Page 23.

**rip:** shortened form of *riptide,* a tide that opposes another or other tides, causing a violent disturbance in the sea. Page 99.

**rolling platform:** a cart with a flat floor, supported on wheels, and with a rack mounted upon it. Clothing can be hung on the rack and thus moved from place to place. Page 65.

**romantic:** relating to the Romantic Movement in English and European literature, art and music, in which writers and artists followed their feelings and emotions rather than logical thought or reason, and preferred wild, natural beauty to things made by people. It was popular in the late eighteenth and early nineteenth centuries. Page 35.

**round out:** complete something in a satisfying or suitable way; bring something to completion. Page 95.

**roustabout:** a deckhand or waterfront laborer. Page 96.

**Royal Air Force:** the British air force, also known by the initials *RAF.* Page 8.

**rude:** rugged; wild. Page 7.

**runner:** a messenger. Page 163.

**running out:** exhausting the negative influence of (something); getting rid of. Page 130.

**saber:** a sword for use by the cavalry (soldiers on horseback) having a curved blade specially adapted for cutting. Page 20.

**sable:** a soft, dark, expensive fur or a garment made of this fur, such as a coat. From the *sable,* a small animal of northern Asia. Page 72.

**saffron:** an orange-yellow spice used for flavoring and coloring food; also, this color. Page 119.

**sage:** a man of deep wisdom, one whose wisdom entitles him to respect. Page 163.

**salt(s):** an informal term for an experienced sailor. Page 23.

**sampling:** converting a sound or a short length of sounds into digital information. This information is stored on a device, such as the Fairlight Computer Musical Instrument (CMI), and can then be manipulated electronically to create desired effects. *See also* **Fairlight.** Page 167.

**sandwich men:** persons with a *sandwich board,* two connected posters or signboards that hang in front of and behind a person and usually bear some advertisement, notice or the like. Page 34.

**sans merci:** a French phrase meaning lacking in or without mercy, from *sans,* without, and *merci,* mercy. Page 119.

**Santa Catalina:** an island lying 20 miles (30 kilometers) off the coast of Southern California. Page 124.

**satire:** a literary work in which vices, follies, stupidities, abuses, etc., are held up to ridicule and contempt. Page 167.

**savant:** a person of extensive learning. Page 131.

**scan, in:** within view. Page 100.

**scepter:** a ceremonial staff, rod or wand used as a symbol of a monarch's authority. Page 109.

**scholastics:** presentation or application of knowledge or learning that is overly concerned with form, minor details or the like and is therefore dry and lifeless. Page 128.

**Scientology:** Scientology is the study and handling of the spirit in relationship to itself, universes and other life. The term Scientology is taken from the Latin *scio,* which means "knowing in the fullest sense of the word" and the Greek word *logos,* meaning "study of." In itself the word means literally "knowing how to know." Page 1.

**score(s):** very many. Literally, a score is a set of twenty. Page 103.

**scowl:** frown in an angry or bad-tempered way. Page 63.

**scuppers:** openings in the sides of a ship that allow water on the deck to drain overboard. Page 23.

**scythed:** cut or mowed something down as if with the sweeping action of a *scythe,* a farming tool with a long, curved blade fastened on a handle, used for cutting down grain, etc., as during a harvest. Page 125.

**seafaring:** of or engaged in life at sea, such as by being a sailor. Page 9.

**Seattle:** a city in west central Washington State in the northwestern US and a major seaport and commercial center. Page 9.

**Secretary of the Navy:** the United States Government official responsible for supervision of all naval affairs. Page 113.

***se faire valoir:*** a French phrase meaning make the most of oneself; show off. Page 123.

**Seine:** a river in France, flowing northwest through Paris to the English Channel, 480 miles (773 kilometers) long. Page 109.

**Senior Officer Present Ashore:** in the navy, an officer who takes command of a group because he holds a higher rank than all other officers present within prescribed geographical limits. Page 113.

**Sentinel Isle:** an island located in the Lynn Canal, a channel between Juneau and Skagway, in southeastern Alaska. Page 104.

**serial:** a motion picture presented in a number of successive installments. Page 2.

**serium:** a coined variation of *serious.* Page 142.

**servitor(s):** a servant or attendant. Page 109.

**shah:** the hereditary monarch of certain Middle Eastern nations; king. Page 79.

**Shakespeare:** William Shakespeare (1564–1616), English poet and dramatist; the most widely known author in all English literature. Page 35.

**shamanic:** of the *shamans,* priests or priestesses who are said to act as intermediaries between natural and supernatural worlds and to use magic to cure ailments, foretell the future and contact and control spiritual forces. Page 8.

**sheepskin:** a university, college or high-school diploma. This term originated in the 1700s and comes from the fact that such documents used to be printed on the skin of sheep prepared as a surface for writing. Page 61.

**shirk:** an instance or the action of *shirking,* avoiding or neglecting something such as work, a duty or responsibility or the like. Page 139.

**showed them:** proved that one was right and made others realize they were wrong. Page 155.

**shroud and spread:** the cloths with which a dead body is wrapped or covered for burial. Page 104.

**Sioux:** also *Dakota,* allied groups of Native North American peoples of the plains of northern United States and adjacent southern Canada. Page 8.

**siren:** in Greek myths, a sea creature, part woman and part bird, who was believed to sing to passing sailors in an enchanting way, in order to lure them to their doom on the rocks she sat on. Page 23.

**Sittin' Bull:** (1834?–1890) Sioux leader Sitting Bull who guided his people to victory against General George A. Custer's cavalry at the Battle of the Little Bighorn (1876). Page 17.

**Skagway:** a port in southeastern Alaska, a commercial and tourist center. Page 103.

**skiff:** a flat-bottom open boat, having a pointed bow and a square stern, propelled by oars, sail or motor. Page 100.

**slot:** a place or position, as in a sequence or series. Page 95.

**smarting:** suffering from or experiencing a sharp, stinging sensation. Page 14.

**smitten:** afflicted with sudden disaster, destruction or injury as if by a hard blow. Page 131.

**sojourn:** a temporary stay. Page 167.

**soundtrack:** a sound accompaniment or music written to accompany (in this case, a book). Page 1.

**spar:** any pole supporting or extending a sail of a ship. Page 27.

**spawn:** (of fish) produce or deposit eggs, sperm or young. Page 108.

**splurge (on):** have or do something enjoyable in great abundance. Page ix.

**spread, purple:** a *bedspread,* an attractive cover put on top of all the sheets and covers on a bed that is *purple,* traditionally the color reserved for the use of a ruler or other royal person. Page 61.

**spread, shroud and:** the cloths with which a dead body is wrapped or covered for burial. Page 104.

**spring sure after brace:** of the rigging (ropes, chains, etc.) on a sailing vessel, to move suddenly (spring) into a stable (sure) position after a *brace,* an action or instance of moving the sail or sails on a ship so as to change the ship's direction by use of ropes, also known as *braces.* On a large ship, bracing is a highly intricate maneuver requiring the majority of the ship's crew due to the immense force involved when the wind is blowing against the sails. Page 23.

**squalors:** conditions of shabbiness and filth resulting from poverty or neglect. Page 129.

**stable(s):** a group or staff of writers engaged to contribute their services when called upon; pool. Page 78.

**Stamboul:** the old city that lies within Istanbul, largest city and chief seaport of Turkey. Lying within walls built in the 400s, Stamboul contains the foremost historical and architectural monuments of Turkey, including Topkapi, the palace of former rulers, and world-famous religious buildings. Page 78.

**stanza:** a group of lines of verse, usually arranged according to a definite plan that can include such things as the number of lines, the way the lines are rhymed and the rhythm. Page 191.

**stave:** break or smash, as by colliding with a rock, reef or the like. Page 107.

**steamer:** a large vessel propelled by one or more steam engines. Page 27.

**steam shovel:** a large machine with a shovel for digging, originally powered by steam. Page 52.

**steeped:** literally, *steeped* means soaked, saturated or bathed in water or a liquid, such as tea in hot water. Used figuratively, it means filled completely with or deeply influenced by. Page 11.

**steepled:** arranged in a form as like a steeple (a tall tower with a pointed roof), such as is shown with fingers placed together and pointed upward in a gesture of prayer. Page 119.

**steeplejack:** a skilled construction worker who performs installations, maintenance and repairs on skyscrapers, towers, steeples, smokestacks and other tall structures. Page 48.

**stenching:** having an extremely strong and disagreeable smell; stinking. Page 11.

**stepladder:** a folding ladder that has broad, flat steps and a hinged supporting frame. A common belief is that a tragedy will happen to someone who walks under a ladder or that it is an unlucky thing to do. Page 78.

**stint:** a period of time spent doing something. Page 113.

**stock:** lacking creative ability or originality; typical. Page 58.

**strand:** a strip of land along the edge of a body of water. Page 79.

**Street & Smith:** a large American publishing company established in the mid-1800s that put out a large number of periodicals and pulp magazines in the late nineteenth and early twentieth centuries, such as *Astounding Science Fiction* magazine and *Unknown* magazine. Page 33.

**strick:** an older form of *struck*. Page 103.

**stricken:** made unfit; damaged. Page 126.

**stunted:** 1. shortened, as if from not having reached a proper height. Page 19.
2. performed dangerous feats in an airplane. Page 48.

**sturgeon(s):** a large fish with a long snout and tough skin, found in northern rivers and coastal waters. Page 149.

**suitor(s):** a man who is trying to persuade a woman to marry him. Page 79.

**summarily:** in a prompt and direct manner; immediately and without delay. Page 95.

**surcease:** relief; a ceasing or end. Page 81.

**sway, bolster (one's):** support and make stronger someone's rule or control over a person, group or area. Page 109.

**swell:** a slow, regular movement of the sea in rolling waves that do not break. Page 99.

**synopsis:** a brief or condensed statement giving a general view of something. Page 8.

**tableau:** a graphic description or visualization; image; picture. Page 84.

**talon:** a claw, especially of a bird of prey. Used as an allusion to a person's grasping hand. Page 109.

**T'ang dynasty:** (618–907) a series of rulers who governed China during this period. It was marked by territorial expansion, the invention of printing and the high development of poetry. Page 35.

**tarango:** a tango (made to rhyme with *fandango*). A *tango* is a dance for couples, originated in South America, with long gliding steps and dips. Page 137.

**tattoo:** a bugle call that tells soldiers to return to their quarters. Page 20.

**tenet(s):** something accepted as an important truth; any of a set of established and fundamental beliefs, such as one relating to religion. Page 138.

**terse:** concise, brief. Page 84.

**testament (to):** something that shows that another thing exists or is true; evidence; proof. Page 180.

***The Sportsman Pilot:*** a monthly American aviation magazine published from around 1930 until 1943. It contained writings on a wide range of subjects, including coverage of aerial sporting events, commentary on current aviation issues, technical articles on flying as well as other articles on topics of general interest. Page 82.

**Thomas Basin:** a boat harbor located at the southern end of Ketchikan, Alaska. A *basin* is an enclosed area of water where boats can be moored. Page 96.

***Thrilling Adventures:*** a pulp magazine produced by the publishing company of Thrilling Publications (also known as Standard Magazines, Beacon Magazines and Better Publications). The company also produced pulp magazines such as *Thrilling Detective, Thrilling Western, Startling Stories* and others. Page 62.

**throng:** a great number of people crowded or assembled together; crowd. Page 20.

**Tilden, Nebraska:** a town in the northeastern part of Nebraska, a state in the central part of the United States. Page 7.

**toast of:** a person who is admired or praised by many people in a particular place. Page 79.

**to horse, to boots and saddles:** get ready for riding by putting on boots, saddling and getting on the horse. Page 20.

**toilsome:** requiring long, hard work. Page 106.

**token, by the same:** in like manner; similarly. Page 58.

**tong and mace:** two weapons, used especially in earlier times. A *tong* is a small ax with a short handle, and a *mace* is a club with a spiked metal head. Page 119.

**tongue, tinkling:** the speaking of pleasant, meaningless words, an allusion to a quote from the Bible: "Though I speak with the tongues of men and of angels, and have not charity [love of fellow human beings], I am become as sounding brass [a brass instrument emitting sound] and the tinkling [meaningless sounds] of the temple bell…I am nothing." Page 121.

**top rankers:** the most successful or respected people in a field or profession. Page 58.

**torpedo, war-headed:** a reference to a *torpedo,* a self-propelled underwater naval weapon with an explosive charge, equipped with an internal-guidance system that controls its direction, speed and depth. *War-headed* refers to the portion of the torpedo filled with explosives, called the *warhead.* Page 98.

**transient:** lasting only a short time; existing briefly; temporary. Page 160.

**travesty:** a crude, distorted or ridiculous representation (of something). Page 81.

**trinket:** a small item of little value; something unimportant. Page 85.

**troglodytic:** characteristic of a *troglodyte,* a person who lives in seclusion. Page 137.

**trooper:** a soldier trained to fight on horseback. Page 20.

**truck light:** a light at the top of a ship's mast. A *truck* is a circular wooden cap fitted to the top of a ship's mast, to which a light (called a *truck light*) is sometimes attached. The light is used for signaling. Page 23.

**turned to clay:** used figuratively, had a hidden or unexpected weakness or frailty. Page 21.

**tutelage:** individual instruction accompanied by close personal attention and a conscious attempt at guidance. Page 7.

**'twas:** a contraction of *it was.* Page 79.

**'twixt:** a shortened form of *betwixt,* an older word meaning between. Page 91.

**two-fisted:** vigorous and virile; also, ready for or inclined to physical combat. Page 58.

**'twould:** a contraction of *it would.* Page 153.

**ukulele:** (shortened form *uke*) a small stringed instrument related to the guitar. It has four strings that are strummed with one hand while the player presses the strings on the neck. The ukulele was developed from a small guitar brought to Hawaii by the Portuguese in the late 1800s. Page 98.

**unafeared:** representing an earlier pronunciation of *unafraid*. Page 20.

**unassuaged:** not having been provided relief, as from something distressing or painful. Page 181.

**unavailing:** being of no use. Page 119.

**undergraduate:** characteristic of or coming from a student at a university or college who has not yet received a degree. Page 8.

**undisputed:** accepted as rightfully deserving the description; unquestioned. Page 33.

**unfettered:** free from restraint; unrestricted. Page 135.

**unpining:** not losing vigor or health due to grief, worry or the like. Page 119.

**unrecompensed:** not having received back something to make up for loss, damage, injury or the like; not repaid. Page 152.

**up-and-coming:** likely to become successful or popular. Page 34.

**urbane:** showing sophistication, elegance, refinement or courtesy. Page 168.

**valiance:** the condition of being *valiant,* meaning showing courage or determination. Page 123.

**van:** a shortened form of *vanguard,* the first or leading position in any field, subject or the like. Literally, the *van* consists of those people occupying the front position in an advancing group; the foremost part of a company of people. Page 129.

**Vancouver:** a city in southwestern British Columbia, Canada, a leading Pacific coast seaport, founded in the mid-1800s. Page 104.

**Vanderbilt Reef:** a *reef* is a ridge of coral or jagged rock in a body of water, with the top just below or just above the surface. The *Vanderbilt Reef* is located 30 miles (48 kilometers) north of Juneau, Alaska, and measures half an acre (21,780 square feet or 2,023 square meters). Page 96.

**verse:** writing that is arranged in lines, often with a regular rhythm or pattern of rhyme; poetry. Page 1.

**vis-à-vis:** in relation to. Page 158.

**vitriolic:** (of language or comments) full of anger and hatred. Page 109.

**wah:** also *wah-wah,* produce a wavering sound on a trumpet by alternately covering and uncovering the wide end of the instrument while blowing into the narrow end. Page 67.

**war-headed torpedo:** a reference to a *torpedo,* a self-propelled underwater naval weapon with an explosive charge, equipped with an internal-guidance system that controls its direction, speed and depth. *War-headed* refers to the portion of the torpedo filled with explosives, called the *warhead.* Page 98.

**Washington (State):** a state in the northwestern United States, on the Pacific coast and bordering with Canada to the north. Page 9.

**watch:** the members of a ship's crew who are on duty at a particular time, usually for a period of four hours. The crew are divided in half with one half, called the *starboard watch,* attending to the working of the ship while the other half, called the *port watch,* are off duty. Page 23.

**waterway, inland:** a natural protected channel (also called *Inside Passage*) in northwestern North America, 950 miles (1,500 kilometers) long. This waterway extends along the coast from Seattle, Washington, past British Columbia, Canada, to the southern area of Alaska. The passage is made up of a series of channels running between the mainland and a string of islands on the west that protect the passage from Pacific Ocean storms. Page 95.

**wax:** take on a specified characteristic or state; become. *Wax enthusiastic* means become enthusiastic. Page ix.

**wayward:** characterized by extreme determination to act in a way that is against what is right, proper or reasonable. Page 108.

**wed:** place in close or intimate association, likened to becoming married. Page 126.

**westing:** westerly progress; a going toward the west. Page 99.

**whaler:** a ship used in *whaling,* the work or industry of hunting and killing whales. Page 9.

**what's that to (someone):** that should not interest (someone). (*What* is used here to introduce a *rhetorical question,* one that is asked for effect rather than to get information.) Page 19.

**wheeled:** turned about in a circular movement, as in a military formation where the inner unit remains in one place, as a pivot, while the outer units make an arc around it. Page 21.

**whence:** from what source, origin or cause. Page 119.

**white collars:** the ranks of office and professional workers whose jobs generally do not involve manual labor or the wearing of a uniform or work clothes. *"White collars walking for lunch money"* alludes to office workers going on foot (instead of paying for transportation) to save money for the purchase of lunch. Page 34.

**whither bound?:** where or to what place, end, point, etc. (are they) going? Page 38.

**Williams, William Carlos:** (1883–1963) American writer and poet, whose use of simple, direct language marked a new course in twentieth-century poetry. Williams was a doctor with his own practice as well as a prolific writer. Page 35.

**wordage:** the quantity or amount of words written, as over a period of time or for a given text, etc. Page 33.

**writhin':** a contraction of *writhing,* moving in a violent twisting or wrenching manner. Page 23.

**wrought:** an older form of *worked,* made or fashioned in a skillful way. Page 33.

**wry:** grimly humorous with a hint of bitterness. Page 7.

**Yangtze:** also *Yang-tze-kiang* (now *Chang Jiang,* meaning *long river*), the world's third-longest river. The river flows from the Tibetan plateau through central China to the East China Sea. Page 8.

**ye:** an old form of *you.* Page 23.

**yea:** indeed; truly. Used to introduce a statement. Page 81.

**yellow bees:** an allusion to the yellow-painted taxis found in great number in New York City. Page 37.

**yer:** an informal variation of *your.* Page 23.

**yon:** that over there, at some distance in the indicated place or direction. Page 120.

**zephyr:** a mild, gentle breeze. Page 13.

# INDEX

# THE
# L. RON HUBBARD
## SERIES

"To really know life," L. Ron Hubbard wrote, "you've got to be part of life. You must get down and look, you must get into the nooks and crannies of existence. You have to rub elbows with all kinds and types of men before you can finally establish what he is."

Through his long and extraordinary journey to the founding of Dianetics and Scientology, Ron did just that. From his adventurous youth in a rough and tumble American West to his far-flung trek across a still mysterious Asia; from his two-decade search for the very essence of life to the triumph of Dianetics and Scientology—such are the stories recounted in the L. Ron Hubbard Biographical Publications.

Drawn from his own archival collection, this is Ron's life as he himself saw it. With each volume of the series focusing upon a separate field of endeavor, here are the compelling facts, figures, anecdotes and photographs from a life like no other.

Indeed, here is the life of a man who lived at least twenty lives in the space of one.

FOR FURTHER INFORMATION VISIT
**www.lronhubbard.org**

To order copies of *The L. Ron Hubbard Series*
or L. Ron Hubbard's Dianetics and
Scientology books and lectures, contact:

US AND INTERNATIONAL

BRIDGE PUBLICATIONS, INC.
*5600 E. Olympic Blvd.*
*Commerce, California 90022 USA*
*www.bridgepub.com*
*Tel: (323) 888-6200*
*Toll-free: 1-800-722-1733*

UNITED KINGDOM AND EUROPE

NEW ERA PUBLICATIONS
INTERNATIONAL ApS
*Smedeland 20*
*2600 Glostrup, Denmark*
*www.newerapublications.com*
*Tel: (45) 33 73 66 66*
*Toll-free: 00-800-808-8-8008*